Battle Above the Clouds

Lifting the Siege of Chattanooga and the Battle of Lookout Mountain

October 16-November 24, 1863

by David A. Powell

EMERGING CIVIL WAR SERIES

Chris Mackowski, series editor
Kristopher D. White, chief historian

The Emerging Civil War Series offers compelling, easy-to-read overviews of some of the Civil War's most important battles and issues.

Recipient of the Army Historical Foundation's Lieutenant General Richard G. Trefry Award for contributions to the literature on the history of the U.S. Army

Other titles in the Emerging Civil War Series include:

The Aftermath of Battle: The Burial of the Civil War Dead
    by Meg Groeling

All the Fighting They Want: The Atlanta Campaign, from Peachtree Creek to the Surrender of the City, July 18-September 2, 1864
    by Stephen Davis

Bushwhacking on a Grand Scale: The Battle of Chickamauga, Sept. 18-20, 1863
    by William Lee White

Calamity in Carolina: The Battles of Averasboro and Bentonville, March 1865
    by Daniel T. Davis and Phillip S. Greenwalt

Grant's Last Battle: The Story Behind the Personal Memoirs of Ulysses S. Grant
    by Chris Mackowski

A Long and Bloody Task: The Atlanta Campaign, from Dalton to Kennesaw to the Chattahooche, May 5-July 18, 1864
    by Stephen Davis

A Want of Vigilance: The Bristoe Station Campaign, October 9-19, 1863
    by Bill Backus and Robert Orrison

For a complete list of titles in the Emerging Civil War Series, visit www.emergingcivilwar.com.

Battle Above the Clouds

LIFTING THE SIEGE OF CHATTANOOGA AND THE BATTLE OF LOOKOUT MOUNTAIN

OCTOBER 16-NOVEMBER 24, 1863

by David A. Powell

EMERGING CIVIL WAR SERIES

SB

Savas Beatie

California

First edition, first printing

ISBN-13 (paperback): 978-1-61121-377-5
ISBN-13 (ebook): 978-1-61121-378-2

Library of Congress Cataloging-in-Publication Data

Names: Powell, David A. (David Alan), 1961- author.
Title: Battle above the clouds : lifting the siege of Chattanooga and the Battle of Lookout Mountain, October 16-November 24, 1863 / by David A. Powell.
Description: First edition. | El Dorado Hills, California : Savas Beatie LLC, 2017. | Series: Emerging Civil War series
Identifiers: LCCN 2017017069| ISBN 9781611213775 (pbk) | ISBN 9781611213782 (ebk.)
Subjects: LCSH: Lookout Mountain, Battle of, Tenn., 1863. | Chattanooga (Tenn.)--History, Military--19th century.
Classification: LCC E475.97 .P69 2017 | DDC 973.7/359--dc23
LC record available at https://lccn.loc.gov/2017017069

SB

Published by
Savas Beatie LLC
989 Governor Drive, Suite 102
El Dorado Hills, California 95762
Phone: 916-941-6896
Email: sales@savasbeatie.com
Web: www.savasbeatie.com

Savas Beatie titles are available at special discounts for bulk purchases in the United States by corporations, institutions, and other organizations. For more details, please contact Special Sales, P.O. Box 4527, El Dorado Hills, CA 95762, or you may e-mail us at sales@savasbeatie.com, or visit our website at www.savasbeatie.com for additional information.

To my father, who set me on this path.

Table of Contents

Footnotes for this volume are available at
http://emergingcivilwar.com/publications/the-emerging-civil-war-series/footnotes

List of Maps

Maps by Hal Jespersen

Acknowledgments

My interest in the battles for Chattanooga stems from my earlier work on the Chickamauga Campaign—which, arguably, is only the first half of the larger campaign for Chattanooga in 1863. That effort lasted three months, involved three major actions and any number of smaller fights, and collectively produced tens of thousands of casualties. Having written extensively on the first act, I decided to turn my attention to the second. This volume is a part of that follow-on effort.

First and foremost, the man I turn to when I have questions that need answering is Chickamauga-Chattanooga National Military Park Historian James H. Ogden III. Jim is indefatigable in his efforts to bring attention to the battles for Chattanooga and a well of information on those battles that never seems to run dry. Fittingly, I have thanked him in every book I've published to date; that is as it should be.

I have made many other friends along the way. Park Interpretive Ranger William Lee White has also been of great help, has become a good friend, is fellow author for the Emerging Civil War series, and is the author of the forward to this volume. When I mentioned the idea of writing a book covering just the fighting for Lookout Mountain, Lee assured me of the need and embraced the concept fully.

Another friend is fellow William Starke Rosecrans enthusiast Dr. Frank Varney of

Even in the 1860s, Lookout Mountain was an iconic tourist site. Looming grandly over the Tennessee River Valley at Chattanooga, thousands of soldiers, both blue and gray, would ascend Lookout's slopes to take in the view. (cm)

Dickinson State University in North Dakota. Frank's insightful essay concerning the Cracker Line contributes greatly to advancing the cause of recognizing General Rosecrans for his very real—and all too often overlooked—contributions towards retaining Union control of Chattanooga in 1863.

I also wish to thank one other invaluable contributor: Harvey Scarborough is the photographer extraordinaire, who supplied many of the modern pictures in this volume. I am not by nature a visually oriented person, and if left to my own devices the images included herein would be notable only for their dull, lifeless nature. Harvey has provided photographs for several of my books. I am indebted to him for his work and for his ever-cheerful, quick turn-arounds of my oft-unreasonable demands.

I am indebted to my colleagues at Emerging Civil War, most especially to Chris Mackowski

The emblem of the Army Corps of Engineers, a castle, served as the inspiration for the entrance to Point Park atop Lookout Mountain at Chattanooga National Battlefield. (cm)

and Kris White, without whom there would be no Emerging Civil War on the web or in print and who enthusiastically supported my suggestion to write a book—two books in fact—on the battles for Chattanooga. They have worked hard to make this project a success. I hope it meets all their expectations.

I wish to also thank the kind folks at Savas Beatie for making this book possible—and not just as publisher of the Emerging Civil War Series. Theodore P. Savas first took a chance on me as a new author in 2009, with *Maps of Chickamauga*, and subsequently gave me the latitude to explore the Chickamauga Campaign in full detail. Ted, along with Sarah Keeney and the rest of the Savas Beatie staff, apply their invaluable skills and talents to making each book a success. I am delighted to be working with them.

Finally, I wish to thank two people who, though neither contributed directly to this book, have been instrumental in their own way. Dr. William Glenn Robertson has always graciously

Cannons and monuments sit atop Orchard Knob. (hs)

shared information and ideas on Chickamauga and Chattanooga. I have learned much from him.

Similarly, I felt myself honored to get to know historian Wiley Sword. I started reading Wiley's work while I was still in high school, and later it was a great honor to get to know and discuss history with him at meetings of the Historians of the Western Theater. Wiley passed on in 2015, but his work lives.

PHOTO CREDITS: Abraham Lincoln Presidential Library (al); *Battles and Leaders* (bl); Bruce F. Bonfield Collection, Brady's National Portrait Gallery (bb); Hamilton County Public Library (hc); *Harper's Weekly* (hw); Library of Congress (loc); Chris Mackowski (cm); National Park Service (nps); *Photographic History of the Civil War* (ph); David Powell (dp); Harvey Scarborough (hs); Tennessee State Library and Archives (tl); US Army (usa); Lee White (lw); Eric Wittenberg (ew)

For the Emerging Civil War Series

Theodore P. Savas, *publisher*
Chris Mackowski, *series editor*
Kristopher D. White, *chief historian*
Sarah Keeney, *editorial consultant*

Maps by Hal Jespersen
Design and layout by H.R. Gordon
Publication supervision by Chris Mackowski

Foreword

BY WILLIAM LEE WHITE

The campaign for Chattanooga in the autumn of 1863 is one of the critical events of the American Civil War. It is also one of the most dramatic and storied chapters of our national epic, the chapter tracing the continued rise of the fortunes of Ulysses S. Grant and the final ignominy of defeat for Braxton Bragg.

The battles set the stage for the changing face of the war that developed on the battlefields of Virginia and Georgia in 1864, where a Confederate army did not face one US Army, but multiple forces. In the case of Chattanooga, Confederates faced not only the Army of Tennessee's old opponent, the Army of the Cumberland, but also elements of Grant's old Army of the Tennessee as well as Joe Hooker's XI and XII Corps of the Army of the Potomac.

From the fighting on the misty slopes of Lookout Mountain to the unyielding surge up the side of Missionary Ridge, the battles around the city—a city President Lincoln considered just as

important as Richmond—became some of the most iconic of the entire war.

The aftermath of the battle of Chickamauga, September 18–20, 1863, set the stage for events two months later, events that included a pseudo siege of Chattanooga and skirmishing both on and off the battlefield by the high commands in both armies. The final result was the highest-fought battle of the Civil War, set atop Lookout Mountain. This battle caused one participant to marvel, "Those who have seen the awe-inspiring precipice at the top of the great mountain can relate what a serious undertaking was before us."

David Powell's *Battle Above the Clouds*, the first of two books, looks at the beginning of the struggle for Chattanooga in the wake of the battle of Chickamauga. It carries us through the iconic battle of Lookout Mountain, famously called "The Battle Above the Clouds," in an engaging and informative manner—one that will be of great value to both a general audience and veteran battlefield trekkers.

"I have gained a great victory and there is none to share
the laurels with me. But Oh! How dear it has cost me.
My dear beloved boy is the sacrifice."

—*John W. Geary, in a letter to his wife, November 2, 1863*

Change of Command

Thursday, October 22, 1863, dawned "clear and warm," a rare break in the near-continuous rains of the past month. The small town of Stevenson, Alabama, overflowed with Federal troops, trainloads of supplies, and all the livestock associated with a great army. Stevenson was the Army of the Cumberland's main supply depot, its streets choked with mountains of material destined for the soldiers all but trapped at Chattanooga, forty-five miles away even by the easiest route. Unfortunately for those Federals, most of those roads were blocked by the Confederate troops. Now each wagonload of critical supplies, so desperately needed in Chattanooga, had to be hauled nearly sixty miles over torturous mountain roads. With too few wagons and teams to accomplish the task properly, the Army of the Cumberland was now living on one-quarter rations, and talk of disaster was in the air.

One of the rail cars that rolled into town that day carried no freight. Instead, it brought Maj. Gen. Ulysses S. Grant and his staff. Grant, the victor of Vicksburg, came bearing the weight of new responsibilities. Six days earlier Grant was assigned command of the newly created

The New York Monument atop Lookout Monument commemorates postwar fellowship. However, events at Chattanooga started on far less cordial note for Federal leadership as well as Confederate leadership. (cm)

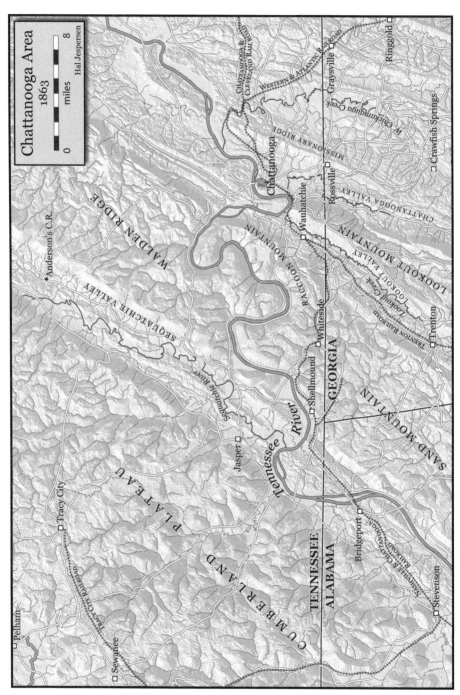

CHATTANOOGA AREA—Chattanooga, encircled by mountains and protected by the Tennessee River, was a daunting objective from any approach.

LEFT: Federal Secretary of War Edwin M. Stanton, who by the fall of 1863 was no supporter of Gen. Rosecrans, played an instrumental role in having Rosecrans replaced. (loc)

RIGHT: The outgoing commander of the Department of the Cumberland, Maj. Gen. William S. Rosecrans, was ostensibly replaced because he threatened to abandon Chattanooga. In fact, neither Stanton nor Ulysses S. Grant was sorry to see Rosecrans depart. (tsla)

Military Division of the Mississippi, charged with overseeing the entire Union war effort between the Mississippi River and the Appalachian Mountain chain. His special charge would be to assume direct command of affairs at Chattanooga. No less an official than the United States Secretary of War, Edwin M. Stanton, requisitioned a special train to meet Grant at Indianapolis to deliver the orders and outline Grant's new duties personally.

Another figure met Grant upon his arrival in Stevenson: Maj. Gen. William Starke Rosecrans, the former commander of the Army of the Cumberland. Upon his disastrous defeat at the battle of Chickamauga the previous month, Rosecrans had lost the confidence of both President Abraham Lincoln and Secretary Stanton. When reports had reached the Federal government in Washington that Rosecrans was thinking of abandoning Chattanooga, Lincoln and Stanton had taken action. Grant's arrival was the result.

When Stanton met with Grant, the war secretary presented him with two copies of the same orders. Each appointed Grant to overall command in the West but with a twist: One retained Rosecrans as commander of the Army of the Cumberland while the other replaced Rosecrans with Maj. Gen. George H. Thomas, Rosecrans's senior corps commander. Unhesitatingly, Grant chose the latter. The telegram relieving Rosecrans

The new man in town was Maj. Gen. Ulysses S. Grant. After Vicksburg, Grant's star was clearly on the rise. In October 1863, authorities in Washington gave him sweeping new authority over the entire Union war effort in the Western Theater. (loc)

Lookout Mountain had once been a bucolic landmark and a popular tourist destination. It now stood as a lynchpin of the Confederate position, dominating Chattanooga below. (loc)

arrived in Chattanooga on October 20. Before dawn the very next morning, Rosecrans quietly departed the city for the long, wet, and muddy ride over Walden's Ridge to Stevenson.

At Stevenson, Rosecrans entered Grant's car to brief him on the Army's circumstances. This meeting could not have been an easy one. There was already bad blood between Grant and Rosecrans dating from when Rosecrans had served as Grant's subordinate in West Tennessee. A series of miscues on Grant's part at the battle of Iuka, in October 1862, left Rosecrans unsupported as he attacked a Rebel force larger than his own, and Rosecrans was not shy about making his displeasure known. For his part, Grant blamed Rosecrans for attacking early. Mutual recriminations created a lingering distrust between the two men.

Despite Washington's fears, Rosecrans had had no intention of abandoning Chattanooga. Instead, his plans had concentrated on re-opening a better supply route into the town via a series of land and water movements, ending his logistics worries. Once re-supplied, Rosecrans could then think about new offensive schemes against his Confederate counterpart, Braxton Bragg. Unfortunately, Assistant Secretary of War Charles A. Dana, sent by Stanton to observe and report on Rosecrans's operations just before the battle of Chickamauga, was the source of a series

The northward view from Lookout Mountain overlooks central Tennessee. During the summer of 1863, Rosecrans's Army of the Cumberland successfully maneuvered Bragg's Army of Tennessee out of the central part of the state and down to the banks of the Tennessee River without hardly firing a shot. Rosecrans urged Lincoln, "[Do] not overlook so great an event because it is not written in letters of blood." Unfortunately, in a case of "what have you done for me lately," Rosecrans's setback at Chickamauga in the fall made it easy for Lincoln to overlook the success of the summer. (cm)

of panicky telegrams informing the outside world that Union retreat was imminent.

Grant greeted Rosecrans cordially enough. Interestingly, Grant informed the other man that he had had no hand in Rosecrans's relief—not true, in fact, for Stanton had left the final decision to Grant. As Rosecrans explained his plans, Grant listened approvingly. Everything made sense and seemed very likely to succeed. The wonder, thought Grant, was that Rosecrans had not already implemented them. It was too late now: Rosecrans was out, and Grant would take over.

Their business concluded, Rosecrans departed. The next day, Rosecrans would board a train northward. Grant traveled on to Chattanooga.

Besieged

CHAPTER ONE

SEPTEMBER 22-OCTOBER 9, 1863

On September 22, 1863, the last Federal troops fell back into the fortified ring encircling Chattanooga from bank to bank on the south side of the Tennessee River. The Army of the Cumberland, badly defeated at the battle of Chickamauga two days before, was much reduced by casualties, now numbering fewer than 35,000 infantry and about 8,000 mounted troops.

By contrast, the opposition—Confederate Gen. Braxton Bragg's Army of Tennessee—had been strongly reinforced, and despite even heavier combat losses, numbered nearly 60,000 of all arms, including 13,000 cavalrymen.

Facing long odds, Major General Rosecrans was reluctantly forced to abandon the dominating summit of Lookout Mountain; he simply did not have enough troops to hold both the town and the surrounding heights. In doing so, he also surrendered control of Lookout Valley, through which ran both the Nashville & Chattanooga Railroad and the main wagon route back to his supply depot at Stevenson.

Though the rail bridge spanning the Tennessee River at Bridgeport had been destroyed back in July, Rosecrans had planned ahead, contracting with builders in Chicago and Cincinnati to repair both that structure and a second bridge at Whiteside, Tennessee—a trestle spanning

One of the most iconic views in all Civil Wardom is the view of Chattanooga from the top of Lookout Mountain. (cm)

WHEELER'S RAID—Unable to bypass Chattanooga with his main army, Braxton Bragg elected instead to send Joseph Wheeler and three Confederate cavalry divisions on a raid deep into Middle Tennessee. Their objective was to sever the rail line between Nashville and Stevenson, Alabama. It was an overly ambitious operation.

The Confederates destroyed the Nashville & Chattanooga rail bridge over the Tennessee at Bridgeport in July 1863 when Braxton Bragg's Army of Tennessee retreated to Chattanooga. Chattanooga's rail connections with the north would not be restored until this bridge was repaired in January 1864. The pontoon bridge seen here under construction was erected by Sheridan's division of the Army of the Cumberland. (loc)

Running Water Creek. But with Confederates occupying Lookout Valley, even if the bridges were speedily rebuilt, neither trains nor wagons could pass through the besieging lines. Another road, rougher but still traversable, ran along the north bank of the Tennessee. However, it was similarly blocked; Rebel sharpshooters posted along the opposite bank wreaked havoc among the Federal teams and drivers, effectively sealing off that route.

Federal troops first marched into Chattanooga on September 9, but there had neither been sufficient transport nor time to shift the all the stockpiled supplies from Bridgeport and Stevenson into the city. By September 21, the Army of the Cumberland had roughly ten days' full rations on hand in Chattanooga, with limited prospects for re-supply. The only remaining unobstructed wagon route between Stevenson and Chattanooga lay over the rugged heights of Walden's Ridge, which dominated the north bank of the Tennessee. Not only did this route require a trip of more than 60 grueling miles, but draft animals had to bring their own forage, limiting the amount of actual supplies that could be transported in each wagonload. This route would have been inadequate to the army's needs under the very best of conditions. With the approach of winter, supplying the army via Walden's Ridge would soon become impossible.

The Federal government's response to this crisis was immediate. Union Maj. Gen. Ambrose Burnside's small Army of the Ohio occupied East Tennessee, headquartered at Knoxville; President Abraham Lincoln's first thought was to order Burnside—who was supposed to be co-operating with Rosecrans in any case—to Chattanooga. Union Quartermaster General Montgomery C. Meigs was also on his way, intent on conducting a personal inspection of the Army of the Cumberland's circumstances.

A second bridge at Whiteside, Tennessee, was also needed to restore Chattanooga's rail link with Nashville. This image of the completed Union trestle, also finished in January 1864, gives some idea of the effort required for that task. Note the blockhouse in the foreground, sited to defend the bridge from guerrillas and raiders. (loc)

Meigs wasted no time, reaching Louisville on September 23 and Bridgeport by the 25th. He arrived at Rosecrans's Chattanooga headquarters the next day after personally traversing Walden's Ridge. "Of the rugged nature of this region," he wired, "I had no conception when I left Washington. I never traveled on such roads before."

Farther afield, on September 22, the Federal War Department also ordered Maj. Gen. Ulysses S. Grant to dispatch as much of his army as could be spared from Mississippi—where it had been resting since the fall of Vicksburg back in July—to Rosecrans's assistance. In turn, Grant immediately ordered his ablest subordinate, Maj. Gen. William T. Sherman, to start moving two divisions eastward. Both Grant and Sherman warned Washington, however, that their movements would take time. After nearly a year's drought in the Ohio, Tennessee, and Mississippi river valleys, low water on those rivers meant slow travel.

As late as October 1, still struggling to ascend the Mississippi to Memphis, Sherman complained that Northern newspapers were falsely claiming that "Rosecrans is already reenforced by Burnside and Sherman. They will doubtless hold us accountable," he sneered, "for not passing by magic from [the] Black River [in Mississippi] to Chattanooga." Instead, thought Sherman, "it will be as much as I expect to get to Memphis tomorrow."

Secretary of War Edwin M. Stanton, an impatient, opinionated man at the best of times, was spurred to even greater efforts. Though Stanton already held Rosecrans in low esteem, he was not ready to give up on Chattanooga. In Virginia, the Union Army of the Potomac had not fought a major engagement with Confederate Gen. Robert E. Lee's forces since Gettysburg. Idle troops, reasoned Stanton, could be sent west.

On September 23, in a hastily called cabinet meeting, Stanton first heard estimates that Burnside's and Grant's forces would take a week to ten days to begin arriving in Chattanooga. Then he dramatically proposed his own solution: transfer 30,000 men from Virginia to Chattanooga, and accomplish the feat within five days. This announcement met with considerable skepticism. Major General Henry Halleck opined that such a move would take more like 40 days. Stanton was prepared, having previously set Col. Daniel C. McCallum, superintendent of the Union Military Railroads, to work on the problem; he now called McCallum in. "The transfer can be begun and fully completed within seven days," the superintendent declared. Stanton was ebullient, the others astounded. "Good! I told you so," shouted Stanton. Then, scowling at Halleck, he added, "Forty days! Forty days indeed, when the life of the nation is at stake!"

Ultimately, two corps—the XI and XII, under the overall command of Maj. Gen. Joseph Hooker—were sent, a force closer to 20,000 than 30,000, but they did indeed begin arriving at Bridgeport within a week's time.

Moreover, as September drew to a close and it became apparent that Braxton Bragg's army would not simply storm into Chattanooga

In September 1863, in response to the logistical crisis at Chattanooga, Union Quartermaster General Montgomery C. Meigs traveled to the region. He was astounded by what he saw, both in terms of the difficulties posed by the terrain and by the innovative spirit on display in the Army of the Cumberland. (loc)

Maj. Gen. William T. Sherman was elevated to command of the Army of the Tennessee when Grant ascended to theater command; he led the forces sent from Mississippi to reinforce Rosecrans in the wake of Chickamauga. (loc)

Confederate General Braxton Bragg led a discontented army in the fall of 1863. Despite the recent victory at Chickamauga, his combat record to date had been mostly one of defeat and retreat. (loc)

immediately, the Federals could work out more deliberate strategies for recouping their losses in southeast Tennessee.

Braxton Bragg also was pondering his options. Confederate logistics presented a limiting factor: Though his army's combat strength had nearly doubled in the past month, with troops arriving from Mississippi and Virginia, none of these reinforcements brought with them their own supply trains. Southern railroad capacity was so limited that even officers coming from Virginia were prohibited from bringing their mounts on the journey. Eventually the wagons were supposed to catch up, but for the immediate future, Bragg's ability to move beyond his railhead was greatly curtailed.

Thus, when on the morning of September 21, flushed with victory and still on the battlefield of Chickamauga, Lt. Gen. James Longstreet proposed a large-scale turning movement across the Tennessee, Bragg rejected the idea. Longstreet proposed shifting the Army of Tennessee north and east, crossing the river between Chattanooga and Knoxville, from whence the Confederates could threaten Rosecrans's massive supply bases at Nashville and Murfreesboro. Given the Confederates' shaky logistics, Longstreet's plan—more of a quickly sketched idea—was never really practical, but Bragg's brusque dismissal of the concept would sew bad blood between the two men. That rejection, however, did not mean that Bragg was content to sit passively outside the Union lines, hoping for the best.

Bragg's victory provided him with something of a dilemma. To be sure, Chickamauga had forced the Federals back into Chattanooga, but there they sat. The larger fruits of that bloody battlefield success had not materialized. For Chickamauga to be truly decisive, Bragg needed Rosecrans to surrender his army, or at the very least fall back to Bridgeport, returning Chattanooga to Confederate control. Within 48 hours, it was obvious that the Federals were going to do neither. Since a frontal assault on the city's fortifications promised only a Confederate bloodbath, Bragg instead sought to tighten the tentacles of what had, by default, become a siege.

* * *

The Army of Tennessee might not be able to sustain itself in Middle Tennessee without a rail connection, but a smaller force could at least raid there. With nearly 13,000 cavalry, Bragg had the means to do exactly that.

Bragg's mounted arm was comprised of two corps, one each commanded by Joseph Wheeler and Nathan Bedford Forrest. This somewhat unorthodox arrangement came about due to the rapid augmentation of Bragg's strength by the accession of the Confederate forces in East Tennessee, expanding Forrest's command from a division to a full corps; and from the fact the oft-disputatious Brigadier General Forrest refused to serve directly under Major General Wheeler.

In the days following Chickamauga, Wheeler's corps operated on the Confederate left, moving toward Bridgeport and securing Lookout Mountain. Forrest led his troops over Missionary

Confederate Lt. Gen. James Longstreet was something of a celebrity in 1863, his fame not yet darkened by the recriminations of Gettysburg that would arise in later years. He and Bragg were destined to butt heads. (b&l)

Ridge, screened the Confederate infantry's approach directly toward Chattanooga, and patrolled the Confederate right, moving up toward the Hiwassee River and Knoxville.

As early as September 22 Bragg ordered both cavalrymen to cross the Tennessee River at various points in order to disrupt Rosecrans's supply line. Various smaller operations, required for sealing off Chattanooga's south bank supply routes, consumed the next few days, and it wasn't until September 28th that Wheeler was ready to execute that mission. On that day, Bragg ordered Forrest to reinforce Wheeler with most of his own corps, placing Wheeler in charge. Forrest, who got along with few people, took leave rather than take orders from Wheeler—a move that suited Bragg. On September 30, after some additional preparation, Wheeler and roughly 8,000 Confederate horsemen crossed the Tennessee River upstream from Chattanooga at Cottonport, to the northeast, in the face of minor opposition from the badly outnumbered 4th Ohio Cavalry.

Wheeler's October Raid, which was also dubbed the First Middle Tennessee Raid (his second would come in August 1864) proved to be a grueling nine-day excursion. On October 1, the gray column scaled Walden's Ridge in the midst of "a heavy downpour . . . the first," noted John Wyeth of the 4th Alabama Cavalry, "we had experienced since . . . August 27th." Camping at the crest, Wheeler's men then descended the eastern face of the ridge on the morning of the 2nd. Here Wheeler divided his forces, sending John Wharton's and Henry B. Davidson's divisions north toward the Union depot at McMinnville, while Wheeler led William T. Martin's division south through the Sequatchie Valley.

At Anderson's Crossroads, Wheeler surprised the tail end of an immense Union supply train (variously estimated as between 400 and 800 wagons) loaded with everything from new uniforms to critical foodstuffs, all headed into Chattanooga. "For fully ten miles . . . we went," recalled Wyeth, "overhauling more wagons, mules and plunder than I ever dreamed of seeing in one day. At times for maybe a quarter or maybe half a mile the road would be clear. Then we would come upon a bunch of from ten to fifteen, or maybe fifty or more wagons, jammed and tangled up in inextricable confusion." The wagons and their contents were torched, the Union mules slaughtered. This victory was heady stuff for the Confederate cavalrymen—and a damaging blow to the Federals.

With smoke of the burning train rising behind him, Wheeler turned north, headed for McMinnville. The Union depot there proved to be equally easy pickings. Facing a force many times his own number, Union Maj. Michael Patterson of the Federal 4th Tennessee Infantry surrendered his 400-man garrison after some preliminary skirmishing. Wharton's troopers paroled the Federals—"Tories" in Confederate eyes—and set about destroying the stores. Patterson's quick capitulation drew much criticism, despite the staunch support of his father-in-law, Union Military Governor Andrew Johnson. "Major Patterson had better call for a court of inquiry in regard to the surrender," warned Army of the Cumberland Chief of Staff James A. Garfield in a telegram dated October 11. "His case may be all satisfactory. We hope so."

Wheeler joined Wharton at McMinnville on October 4. Re-united, Wheeler intended to move his whole force west toward the all-important Nashville & Chattanooga Railway. Federal cavalry was already in pursuit, led by Maj. Gen. George Crook; the National force included Crook's own division and Col. John T. Wilder's mounted infantry brigade. Ahead, other Federals were gathering to defend strategic points along the rail line. On October 5, Wheeler's column skirted the defenses of Murfreesboro. Here, the earthworks of Fortress Rosecrans defended a major Union supply depot whose loss would have been very damaging to the Army of the Cumberland;

Maj. Gen. Joseph Wheeler was a professional soldier from the West Point class of 1859. However, his record as Bragg's cavalry commander proved mixed. His repeated failings during September 1863 left Bragg blind to Union movements and precipitated the Confederate withdrawal from Chattanooga on September 9. (tsla)

Union cavalry commander George Crook led the pursuit of Wheeler through Middle Tennessee. When he caught up with the Confederates on October 7, he delivered a stinging defeat to them at Farmington. (loc)

however, the fortifications were too strongly held to capture easily. Instead Wheeler concentrated on destroying the rail line around town, burning or chopping down bridges and tearing up track. This activity continued through the next day as Wheeler followed the rails toward Wartrace, 25 miles to the south. On the afternoon of the 6th, Wheeler's column broke away from the rail line, moving west to Shelbyville, going into camp along the south bank of the Duck River.

The Federal response gathered momentum. Elements of Hooker's arriving force were diverted to help strengthen the railroad garrisons, with other men set to work repairing the destruction. An additional several thousand infantrymen deployed along the tracks also meant that Wheeler would not be able to slip back eastward undisturbed.

Meanwhile, the pursuing Union cavalry were gaining. Things came to a head on the morning of October 7, when Crook's cavalry surprised Henry Davidson's division of Rebels west of Shelbyville, striking the Confederates just as they stirred from their camps. The result was a running fight, with Davidson's men badly routed. Other Confederates made a stand outside of the small village of Farmington, barely staving off the aggressive blue-clad cavalry until Wheeler could extricate his supply wagons from the closing Federal trap. Though Wheeler would use his escape as reason to claim a victory at Farmington, in truth, he was roughly handled, losing significantly in both men and material. Only Federal miscommunication prevented the disaster from being complete, as one of George Crook's orders to a subordinate brigade went astray, opening for Wheeler an escape route to the south.

The Farmington fight effectively ended Wheeler's excursion. His cavalry turned south and rode hard for Alabama, crossing to the south bank of the Tennessee River two days later. Both men and beasts were exhausted from their constant travails. A supporting movement by Confederate Brig. Gen. Phillip D. Roddy out of Northern Alabama also came to naught.

Part of the reason for the Confederate cavalry's defeat at Farmington was indiscipline, which had become rife. Wheeler's command suffered serious desertion problems during the raid, and many of the troops indulged in indiscriminate looting. The Confederate cavalry "are . . . said to have committed many depredations upon the citizens," reported one Georgia newspaper, taking whatever pleases their fancy, whether from friend or foe." In his own report of the mission, Wheeler found it necessary to admit, damningly, that "many men were allowed by their officers to throw away their arms to enable them to bring out private plunder."

Equally seriously, the grueling pace of the ride broke down many animals, leaving far too many Rebel horse soldiers afoot. Since Confederate practice allowed cavalrymen to own their mounts, granting them furloughs to seek new stock when needed, a lost or un-rideable horse often meant the

Lookout Mountain was a popular tourist destination before the war, and soldiers from both sides visited at various times during 1863-64 (such as those here at Twin Sisters Rock). During the siege of Chattanooga, though, Lookout went from a tourist destination to a vital point in the Confederate position. (loc)

loss of a man, as he went home to find a new animal in an increasingly livestock-scarce Confederacy.

Though the raid cost Wheeler a large number of men through combat, desertion, or the loss of horseflesh, it was not entirely unsuccessful. The destruction of the Union train at Anderson's Crossroads was a major blow to Rosecrans's logistics, and the damage inflicted on the Nashville & Chattanooga delayed Hooker's movement by a week or more. Both of those results proved deleterious to the Union circumstances in Chattanooga. Nature, however, would soon deliver the harshest blow yet.

On Location: Visiting sites involved in the Federal supply routes

Though the various locations mentioned in this chapter are widely scattered, they offer the ambitious traveler many rewards, both scenic and historic. (See the first driving tour for directions and details.)

The towns of Stevenson and Bridgeport Alabama, so critical as supply depots to the Union army, both have historical points of interest today. Stevenson has a rail depot museum (though the building is postwar), a Union earthwork built to defend the depot—Fort Harker, named after a Union officer killed in 1864—and the ruins of Rosecrans's headquarters before the Chickamauga campaign: "The Little Brick." Bridgeport also has a city museum worth visiting.

To gain a better appreciation of the difficult nature of the terrain surrounding Chattanooga, the determined visitor can make his way to Signal Point, a small reservation of the Chickamauga-Chattanooga National Military Park. While it is out of the way, the views are spectacular, and the adventurous can hike down to the Tennessee River.

New Arrivals

CHAPTER TWO

THE UNION LINES
OCTOBER 1-24, 1863

For the Army of the Cumberland, more damaging than raiders was the turning of the season. The hot, dry summer of 1863 was over, and with it, the end of a long drought. As October arrived, so did steady rains.

On October 1, as Sherman toiled up the Mississippi and Private Wyeth of the Alabama Cavalry was enjoying the first of these rainfalls, Quartermaster General Montgomery Meigs —now in Chattanooga—also reported what he thought was good news: "Rain at last; truly grateful in laying the dust, which has become a serious affliction to this army. The river rises." The rising river also meant that if Lookout Valley could be returned to Union control, steamboats could begin hauling supplies between Bridgeport and Chattanooga, effectively ending Union supply worries.

Unfortunately, meteorological conditions were about to swing from one extreme to the other. Lieutenant Charley Mosman of the 59th Illinois also noted October 1st's rain, so heavy it was "coming down in torrents . . . [which] fills our trenches with water." Next came a cold front, followed on October 12 by another storm. This time, the rain fell for four days straight, often in sheets. On the 13th, Mosman noted, "it rained . . . so hard we could scarcely keep

Though a post-war construction, this depot sits on the site of the wartime train station in Bridgeport. In October 1863, the streets here would have been crowded with troops and stacks of supplies. (cm)

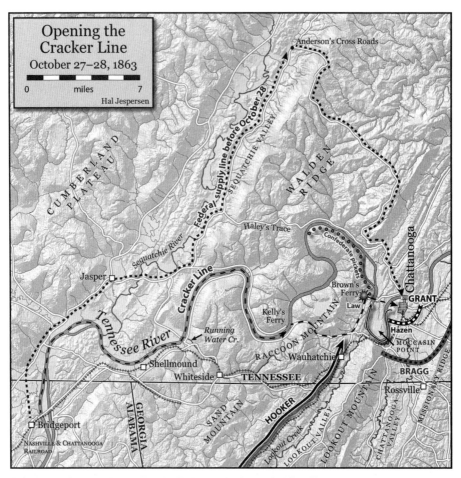

OPENING THE CRACKER LINE—For the Federals, the key to holding Chattanooga was in restoring a reliable supply line to the outside world. With the railroad bridges down, only the river offered a viable alternative. Though rapids and low water prevented boat traffic from steaming all the way to Chattanooga's docks, Kelly's Ferry proved a viable alternative. From there supplies could be hauled overland much more easily.

the fire going." By the 15th, "everybody was out of humor, in fact, from expressions used they were all swearing mad."

Intermittently heavy precipitation continued for the rest of the month. By October 22, Pvt. William Boddy of the 92nd Illinois Mounted Infantry noted how everything had become "very muddy." The next day, Boddy continued, it was "very rainy, wet, cold, and disagreeable and what is worse, our rations are getting very short, and forage . . . can scarcely be obtained at all."

Boddy was not the only one noticing the ration cut. In fact, Boddy's regiment had it better than most, stationed as it was on the north bank of the Tennessee upstream from Chattanooga, and dispersed far enough to the north that they could secure some forage locally. For the men manning the defenses of Chattanooga, things were growing pinched. The army's supply route over Walden's ridge, already insufficient, was now churned to loblolly and rendered nearly impassable. The 36th Illinois regimental history noted that in October, "it seemed as though the very heavens had turned to water. . . . The sixty miles between Chattanooga and Bridgeport required a longer time with every trip, and the animals grew more and more exhausted with incessant labor and lack of forage. . . . [T]he rations served out to the men were steadily reduced. The possibility of being starved out . . . stared us in the face."

Though a turn-of-the-20th-century structure, Stevenson's Depot sits about where the historic depot did. It was once a frantic place, swarming with activity day and night. (dp)

And this was only the beginning. Winter loomed, and with it the promise of even more bad weather. The Union army's already precarious situation would only continue to worsen.

Back in late August, General Rosecrans's chief engineer, Brig. Gen. James St. Clair Morton, expressed his desire to leave the army. That transfer was still pending at the time of the battle of Chickamauga, where Morton was slightly wounded in the hand. The ensuing crisis postponed his departure, but on September 30, his replacement as chief engineer arrived.

William F. "Baldy" Smith was a West Pointer. He graduated 4th in his class of 1845, which granted him access to the ante-bellum army's elite corps of engineers, where he did well. A Vermonter, he transferred to volunteer service when war came, but was soon made a general in the Army of the Potomac. He served as a divisional commander before assuming command of the VI Corps during

By the summer of 1863, William F. Smith was just another Union general watching the war from the sidelines, benched for his outspoken, imprudent meddling in army politics. The transfer westward, however, gave him a shot at career redemption. (loc)

the Fredericksburg campaign. There, he unwisely chose to involve himself in the tangled politics of that army, undermining army commander Ambrose E. Burnside in a letter to President Lincoln. As a result, he lost command of his corps, his appointment to major general was refused by the Senate, and he soon found himself benched. He commanded militia during the Gettysburg crisis. However, fortune smiled upon him once again that fall, for his engineering acumen made him a logical choice to supersede Morton.

Smith would later take much credit for saving the army, arriving at the moment of crisis in Chattanooga, sizing up the situation, and devising the plan that would restore the army to full rations by taking control of Lookout Valley. Rosecrans, he asserted, had nothing to do with it. Smith publicized his own role in the events of October 1863 in both the popular postwar press and, at the turn of the century, to the park commissioners of the newly created Chickamauga-Chattanooga National Military Park—so much so, in fact, that in 1901, a military review board was empaneled to pass judgment on Smith's assertion "that the plan to re-open the river line was his and not General Rosecrans's."

In reality, Rosecrans's plans were already well developed when Smith arrived. On September 27, Rosecrans laid out the basic concept for General Meigs. New steamboats were already under construction at Stevenson, and several of the boats captured or sunk when Chattanooga fell into Union hands were now being raised and repaired. When the transports were ready, Hooker's arriving infantry would be used to seize control of Lookout Valley. This step would allow the Federals to throw pontoon bridges across the Tennessee at Chattanooga and at some likely place west of Lookout Mountain. As the river rose, the completed steamboats would haul supplies between Stevenson, Bridgeport, and the landing at Kelly's Ferry. Kelly's Ferry lay on the south bank of the Tennessee River west of Raccoon Mountain. From there, a good road led six miles through Cummings Gap to either

Camps at Stevenson

George H. Blakeslee, a soldier in the 129th Illinois, sketched this view of a Union camp and fort at Stevenson, Alabama, on his way south in March of 1864. (loc)

Brown's Ferry or the mouth of Lookout Creek, where, via pontoons, it was only another 2-3 miles into Chattanooga.

Rosecrans's plan depended on three essential elements: the availability of the steamboats, the arrival of sufficient reinforcements to seize and hold Lookout Valley, and the completion of enough pontoons to bridge the river twice. Each component had to be in place before he could act.

The new steamboats were of simple design, nothing more than "an engine, a boiler, and a stern-wheel on a flat bottomed scow," but they would serve the Federals well. Rosecrans pre-planned for five boats, shipping the vital machinery south to Stevenson via the rails, but eventually a dozen vessels would be built there. Rosecrans also hired a man known only to the record as Mr. Turner, an experienced boat-builder from the Great Lakes, to oversee construction. The 1st Michigan Engineers & Mechanics provided the bulk of the labor. They completed the first boats around the second week of October, which is when Rosecrans began pressing Maj. Gen. Joseph Hooker to move into Lookout Valley.

This image, which dates from 1864, depicts Cameron Hill on the right, with Lookout Mountain looming directly behind, and a number of fortifications defending the city. Close inspection reveals a train rounding the foot of Lookout from the far right. (hw)

Joseph Hooker was also a controversial figure, come west to reclaim a reputation. Like William F. Smith, he had immersed himself in army politics, though where Smith was benched for his undermining of Burnside, Hooker replaced Burnside. Unlike most Regular Army officers, Hooker made himself popular with both politicians and political generals. He was a favorite among the Radical Republican element in Congress. Thus, even after Hooker's shattering defeat at Chancellorsville in May of 1863, Lincoln did not relieve him of command, even though he had lost the confidence of both the president and Secretary Stanton. Hooker's replacement came only when he himself offered to resign on June 28—a move calculated to grant him more freedom of action, although it backfired, and Hooker was summarily replaced by Maj. Gen. George Gordon Meade just three days before what turned out to be the biggest battle of the war: Gettysburg.

Still, Hooker was a ranking major general with considerable political clout. He was therefore chosen to command the combined XI and XII Corps sent to reinforce Rosecrans. This appointment pleased neither Maj. Gens. Oliver O. Howard nor Henry W. Slocum, who commanded those two corps. Hooker blamed Howard and his XI Corps for effectively

Joseph "Fighting Joe" Hooker was another officer looking for redemption, though his conglomerate of a command was not a happy one. (loc)

George Thomas was a brigadier general. Thomas reluctantly assumed authority over the Army of the Cumberland after it was apparent that Rosecrans would not remain in command. (loc)

Joe Hooker blamed General Howard for the Union disaster at Chancellorsville. So, too, did most of the men in the XI Corps, upon which the shattering attack of May 2, 1863, had fallen. As a result, Howard was favored neither from above nor below. (loc)

Gen. Henry Slocum, commanding the XII Corps, was exceedingly displeased to be serving under Hooker again; Slocum's tenure under Hooker during the Chancellorsville campaign had been an unhappy one. In an attempt to avoid serving under Hooker again, Slocum would ask for a transfer rather than continue on to Chattanooga with his corps. (loc)

losing the battle of Chancellorsville through neglect and incompetence, while the pious Howard found Hooker both morally and militarily inadequate. Slocum also fumed over the Chancellorsville debacle, and to make matters worse, felt that he should have been given command of this new expedition in Hooker's stead.

Whatever simmering animosity lay between the three men, it did not impede the transfer. The first XI Corps men detrained in Bridgeport on the afternoon of September 30, meeting Stanton's self-imposed deadline, the promised seven-day timetable. Howard arrived on October 2, assuming command of the post. Hooker reached Stevenson the next day, in response to Rosecrans's wire of September 30 directing that officer to "come on with all dispatch . . . and assume command there." A steadily growing force of infantry soon reached 10,000, rendering both Stevenson and the smaller depot at Bridgeport, five miles east, secure from any sudden Rebel strike.

That blue flood was suddenly interrupted when Joe Wheeler's Confederate cavalry descended on the Nashville & Chattanooga tracks between Murfreesboro and Shelbyville. While the damage inflicted was moderate, it did slow Hooker's movement in two ways: by diverting a division of the XII Corps to guard duty between Nashville and Stevenson, and in halting the onward shipment of Hooker's supply wagons.

A nineteenth-century army was no less road-bound than any modern force—perhaps more. While the bulk of the men moved on foot, the ammunition, food and other material that kept such a force functioning required wagons. The standard US Army wagon hauled twenty-five hundred

This sketch of the steamboat *Chattanooga* at Kelly's Ferry shows just how rudimentary these boats were: little more than rafts with engines—but they served their purpose. (b&l)

pounds with a six-mule team; field ambulances required four-horse teams. In 1862, the Army of the Potomac maintained a ratio of 49 wagons per 1000 men—and that while operating only a relatively short distance from its base—rails were plentiful in Virginia. This figure would be constantly reduced in an effort to make the various field columns more mobile (by 1864, the figure was 34 per thousand) but even so, Hooker's combined force required something like 500 wheeled vehicles of various types. As of early October, all of these vehicles were still in transit, mostly still north of the Ohio River. In wire communications with Rosecrans, as late as October 22, Hooker cited his lack of wheeled transport as the primary reason delaying his movement into Lookout Valley. The one benefit of Wheeler's raid was that Slocum, who had no desire to serve under Joe Hooker ever again, remained at Murfreesboro to command the troops detailed for rail guard duties.

* * *

If Wheeler's cavalry had not raided Middle Tennessee that October, perhaps William Starke

Rosecrans would have had a chance to implement his plan before he was relieved of command. Or perhaps not: even if Hooker's movement were uninterrupted, there was still the need for both the steamboats and the pontoons being ready. Until all the elements of the plan were in place, initiating the movement to re-open Chattanooga's supply line would be premature, telegraphing Union intentions to the Confederates and giving them time to react before those all-important first boatloads of rations reached Chattanooga.

Wagons were the lifeblood of army logistics. This image shows a mix of army ambulances, standard six-horse wagons, and other vehicles all needed to keep a force moving on campaign. (loc)

Rosecrans's relief was made fact before the plan became action. The order removing him arrived in Chattanooga on October 19. Rosecrans departed early on the 20th, making the difficult journey over Walden's Ridge and down through Sequatchie Valley. On the 22nd, Rosecrans and Grant had their fateful meeting at Stevenson.

Grant now began his own arduous journey to Chattanooga, traversing those same roads over Walden's Ridge in reverse. Grant, whose left leg was still sore from when a horse fell on him in New Orleans on September 4, now re-injured that bad leg when his mount fell again, slipping in the mud while ascending Walden's Ridge. Despite the mishap, Grant reached the Army of the Cumberland's headquarters shortly after dark on October 23, where he met with George Thomas.

Lieutenant Colonel James H. Wilson, a topographic engineer on Grant's staff, later described this first meeting between the two men as difficult, with both Grant and Thomas seemingly "glum and ill at ease." Wilson preceded his commander into town, spending the night of October 22 with his friend Capt. Horace Porter, who was an ordnance officer on Thomas's staff. When they heard that Grant had arrived, both

Grant's reception at Thomas's headquarters has been depicted as lacking in warmth. Despite the import of that meeting, however, there are only two contemporary written descriptions of the moment. (nps)

men bustled to Thomas's headquarters on Walnut Street, where they found Grant sitting before the fireplace, "steaming from the heat over a small puddle which had run from his sodden clothing." Wilson thought Thomas was intentionally snubbing Grant, perhaps resentful of the fact that Grant had been promoted over himself, and at Rosecrans's expense. Porter thought otherwise. "General Thomas's mind had been so intent upon receiving the commander, and arranging for a conference of officers, that he had entirely overlooked his guest's travel-stained condition." Once an aide pointed out the condition of Grant's apparel, Thomas offered Grant a change of clothes, which the latter refused. Wilson also recalled that Grant was offered nothing to eat until he himself suggested it, but Porter noted that Grant had already "partaken of a light supper immediately after his arrival."

While the specific differences in the two accounts are fairly minor, the suggested tone is quite different. Wilson's account gives the impression of Thomas being cold and aloof, almost sulking, while Porter suggests nothing of the sort. If Grant was offended, he did not say so in writing, and both Wilson's and Porter's accounts first appeared many years after the two principals were long dead. Porter's memoir appeared in 1897; Wilson's, 1912. Alas, no one seems to have left anything like a contemporary account of this fateful first meeting. Assistant Secretary of War Charles A. Dana, who was also present, merely wired Secretary Stanton that Grant had arrived, "wet, dirty, and well."

Matters soon turned to strategy. Between the time of Rosecrans's departure on October 20 and Grant's appearance on the evening of the 23rd, "Baldy" Smith secured Thomas's approval to continue preparations for implementing the re-supply plan. Smith had been surveying the banks of the Tennessee, seeking a suitable site for the second leg of the supply route between Kelly's Ferry and wherever the Tennessee could best be bridged west of Lookout Mountain. In the end, Smith liked Brown's Ferry for this operation much better than the mouth of Lookout Creek, not the least for the range of high hills lining the south bank at that point. If they could be seized and fortified quickly, it would secure the bridge site from any rapid Rebel counterstroke. By the time Grant reached town, Smith asserted, "the plan for opening the river had been matured." Smith and others of Thomas's staff now began to lay out the plan systematically for their new boss.

Grant listened attentively. Porter recalled that "Grant sat for some time as immovable as a rock and as silent as the sphinx," digesting it all. Then he "straightened himself up . . . his features assumed an air of animation, and . . . [manifesting] a deep interest in the discussion, he began to fire whole volleys of questions at the officers present." With those questions, thought Porter, Grant demonstrated "the quickness of his perception" and a deep knowledge of the army's condition. The plan reviewed and approved, Grant made arrangements to personally survey the Union lines the next morning, and, after writing some dispatches, turned in.

Originally one of Thomas's staff officers, Horace Porter first met Grant in Chattanooga. The two took to each other immediately. (loc)

Dissension in the Ranks

CHAPTER THREE

THE CONFEDERATE LINES

OCTOBER 1-24, 1863

While profound changes were taking place within the Union high command, Confederate Gen. Braxton Bragg was grappling with problems of his own.

On paper, the Army of Tennessee should have been riding an emotional high that October. Chickamauga, after all, was one of the more decisive tactical successes of the war—a third of the enemy army routed off the field, including the opposing army commander and two of his corps commanders. Among the trophies of victory were nearly 5,000 prisoners and somewhere between 36 and 51 cannon, depending on who was doing the tallying.

And yet, a month on, for most of the men in the ranks, it didn't feel much like a resounding victory. Chattanooga was still in Union hands, Rebel prospects for resuming the offensive were limited, and even Bragg's own supply situation on Missionary Ridge was precarious.

Then there was the matter of internal dissent. By the fall of 1863, the Army of Tennessee—long a simmering stewpot of resentment, back-biting, jealousies and bitterness—threatened to boil over completely. Bragg was unpopular with many of his generals, including most of his senior subordinates. Long-standing conflicts with corps commanders Leonidas Polk and William J. Hardee—transferred to Mississippi that summer—were now augmented

By October 1863, Braxton Bragg had commanded the Army of Tennessee for sixteen months. Despite several near-successes, Bragg had yet to deliver a clear-cut battlefield victory. His army was riddled with internal strife. (tsla)

Joseph E. Johnston was the fourth-most-senior full general in the Confederate Army—a point that rankled him. He thought he should have been second. Given the problems within the Army of Tennessee, he should have replaced Bragg long ago. He might have commanded in Chattanooga in Bragg's stead. (loc)

by dissension from new players, James Longstreet, Simon B. Buckner, and Daniel Harvey Hill.

The roots of this conflict went back a year, to the Kentucky campaign. Bragg inherited command of the army after the battle of Shiloh, when Southern fortunes in the Western Theater appeared to be irreversibly waning. In an impressive feat of strategy and logistics, Bragg jointly embarked, along with the East Tennessee forces of Maj. Gen. Edward Kirby Smith, on an offensive campaign into Kentucky, which culminated at the battle of Perryville.

Perryville was a mismatched blunder of a battle, in which Bragg directed Polk and Hardee—with 15,000 troops between them—to attack the much larger Union Army of the Ohio, roughly 50,000 strong. Bragg insisted on this attack because he misread the military tea-leaves. He believed the Federals at Perryville to be only a diversionary column. Much of his remaining force, along with Kirby Smith's men, were positioned closer to Frankfort. Bragg intended for Polk and Hardee to quickly crush the supposedly small force facing them and then come join him for what would be the real battle over Kentucky. Both Polk and Hardee protested the order, which they knew to be foolhardy. Bragg would not be dissuaded. At Bragg's personal insistence, they finally initiated that attack on the afternoon of October 8, 1862.

Fortunately for the outnumbered Rebels, the Federals matched Bragg blunder for blunder. Union army commander, Don Carlos Buell, couldn't conceive that the Rebels might attack him. When they did, poor communications between Buell and his subordinates meant that two thirds of the Union force didn't get into action. The remaining third was badly mauled by the attacking Confederates, who nearly routed the Union corps under Alexander McDowell McCook.

By day's end, Bragg realized his mistake and fell back toward Danville, hoping to unite his army and renew the fight. Once he reached Danville, however, instead of seeking to renew the action on more equal terms, Bragg instead decided to leave Kentucky entirely. His army was confused by the abrupt decision to retreat. Even though the strategic fruits of the Kentucky campaign were significant—stabilizing the Western Theater for the next six to nine months and postponing the fall of Chattanooga for a year—the campaign's sour ending left many of Bragg's subordinates disheartened and disillusioned.

There followed a short interlude, as both Federals and Confederates regrouped. In early December, President Jefferson Davis called Kirby Smith, Bragg, Hardee, and Polk to Richmond to confer. Smith, Bragg, and Polk each held interviews with the President. Hardee begged off but sent a lengthy letter instead. Though Smith, Polk, and Hardee all aired their objections to Bragg's leadership and expressed the desire to see Bragg replaced by Joseph E. Johnston, Davis ignored their concerns—even Polk's concern despite the fact that he, a former West Point roommate of the Confederate president's, had up to that time been a confidante and trusted advisor. Bragg and his corps commanders returned to the Army of Tennessee, stationed in and around Murfreesboro, 30 miles from Nashville.

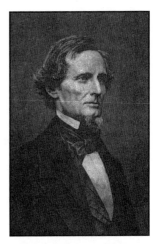

Jefferson Davis, alarmed at what amounted to mutiny within the ranks of the Army of Tennessee's commanders, hurried to the front in October. His presence failed to resolve any of the rancor. (loc)

Federal President Abraham Lincoln, not satisfied with Buell's performance, had in the meantime appointed a new man to command the Army of the Ohio: Maj. Gen. William S. Rosecrans. Just after Christmas, Rosecrans led his men out against Bragg. When the two forces met for battle on December 31, 1862, both armies were more evenly matched, numbering roughly 40,000 men apiece. Deployed along the banks of Stones River, both generals planned to assail their opponent's right wing, but Bragg struck first. Again the blow fell on Alexander McCook, and again, his corps crumpled under the weight. The Federals rallied in the afternoon, avoiding destruction, but only just. Casualties were heavy.

New Year's Day saw a pause, and then Bragg tried one more assault late on January 2. This last attack was poorly conceived, sending a lone division against the Union left. It accomplished nothing except to further augment the sense of discontent among the Rebel officer corps. After another day's pause, Bragg retreated south toward Tullahoma and Shelbyville, allowing Rosecrans to claim the field and a victory.

This retreat also came as a shocker, especially coming on the heels of dispatches issued on December 31, touting Rebel successes. Criticism of Bragg, much of it originating within the Army of Tennessee, now rose to a fever pitch in the popular press.

There now came another, lengthier pause in operations. Both sides spent the first half of 1863

While with the army, Davis toured the battlefield at Chickamauga and visited army camps. He delivered several orations, including one from here, Pulpit Rock on Lookout Mountain. This image was taken in 1864, when it was the scene of a Union signal station. (loc)

preparing for future campaigns. The Federals occupied Nashville and Murfreesboro; the Rebels faced them in a defensive line stretched between Shelbyville and Tullahoma. Raids and small clashes marked the months between January and June 1863, but no major battle resulted.

During much of this period, the Army of Tennessee seethed with internal conflict. Bragg foolishly initiated the fight when, in late January, responding to charges that he retreated at Murfreesboro against his corps commanders' wishes, the commanding general issued an astounding document: a circular addressed to all his senior officers, polling them not only about what they recollected of that decision to withdraw but whether they retained confidence in Bragg's ability to command the army. If not, Bragg offered, he would resign. Oblivious as to the depth of his subordinates' dissatisfaction, Bragg was astounded when he discovered that, in fact, he did not retain their confidence.

Even then, Bragg, ever deaf to the political currents, continued to believe that this dislike was not widespread, just confined to a few troublesome generals. Instead of resigning, Bragg moved to quell that dissent. Before he could act, Joseph E. Johnston arrived at headquarters, charged by President Davis to investigate the problem and resolve it.

Johnston had his own baggage. For one, he did not get along well with Davis, who viewed Johnston as too cautious, unwilling to take the offensive. Johnston had commanded the south's principal army in Virginia until he was wounded outside of Richmond in May 1862. His replacement was Robert E. Lee, a man far more to Davis's liking who won immediate offensive successes with the newly re-christened Army of Northern Virginia. Johnston resented being replaced. Now Johnston had nominal command of the vast western theater, a position he felt was poorly defined. More than anything, Johnston wanted a field command and a chance to prove himself anew.

But not at the perceived expense of another. Hyper-sensitive on matters of honor, Johnston worried that if he investigated the troubles within Bragg's army only to assume personal command of it, he would be seen as scheming to replace Bragg from the onset. As a result, in his first report to Davis shortly after reaching the Army of Tennessee in late January, Johnston bolstered Bragg: the army was fine, discipline was good, and the dissent was confined to a few malcontents.

Johnston had come to the army with private assurances from Confederate Secretary of War James Seddon that he had the government's (really, President Davis's) support in removing Bragg to take personal command. Instead, Johnston's decision to back Bragg allowed Bragg to lash out against several officers whom Bragg believed had performed poorly at Murfreesboro, officers including John C. Breckinridge. Breckinridge, a Kentuckian, already blamed Bragg for the failures of the October campaign, and now Breckinridge was being scapegoated for mismanagement at Murfreesboro.

By March of 1863, Johnston's papering-over of the problems in January allowed the crisis to mushroom into near mutiny.

Again Davis dispatched Johnston to Bragg's headquarters, arriving on March 9, 1863. This time, Johnston was not there merely to investigate: President Davis explicitly ordered him to relieve Bragg of command. Bragg would report to Richmond for further orders.

When he arrived, Johnston found Bragg's wife critically ill. Astoundingly, Johnston refused to take command, citing that now would not be a good time for a change in leadership.

Lookout Mountain made an impressive observation post. This Confederate signal station overlooked the west side of the Mountain, down into Wauhatchie and Lookout Valley. (loc)

Johnston remained with the army from mid-March until early May, but his presence did nothing to resolve the rift. In April, once Bragg's wife's recovered, Johnston protested that now his own ill health prevented him from relieving Bragg and assuming command. Finally, Davis ordered Johnston to Mississippi, where the spring campaigning season opened and brought with it another crisis: Vicksburg.

Bragg might have weathered the storm, but he failed to win over any of his enemies. Active operations resumed in June, and there was no time for overt feuding. Unfortunately for the Army of Tennessee, the summer of 1863 saw only continued defeat. In late June, William Rosecrans launched a brilliant turning movement, designed to flank Bragg out of his strong positions south of Murfreesboro. Despite near-constant rain, Rosecrans succeeded in throwing Bragg off balance, and once again, the Confederates retreated—this time all the way back to Chattanooga. Middle Tennessee, the most productive and most pro-Confederate part of that state, was now firmly in Union hands.

Hardee was transferred to Mississippi, replaced by Daniel Harvey Hill. Hill, once a rising star in the Army of Northern Virginia, had been quietly eased out of that army in late 1862, sent away at the request of Robert E. Lee himself, who found Hill's querulous pessimism annoying. Why President Davis supposed Hill would get along any better with Bragg is a mystery. Davis also sent Maj. Gen. Thomas C. Hindman to Bragg, after Hindman alienated too many Arkansans with his high-handed command style. Given their past histories, both were poor choices for an army already wracked by rancor. Neither man would do much to quell the ongoing spirit of turmoil within Bragg's army.

Then came September and another Union offensive movement—this time for control of Chattanooga. Again Rosecrans resorted to a flank move, and again, Bragg fell back. As had been pre-arranged, Simon B. Buckner—then commanding the quasi-independent Department of East Tennessee—joined Bragg in that movement since Buckner's own command was under threat from yet another Federal force coming from Eastern Kentucky.

The loss of Chattanooga galvanized the Confederacy to send Bragg reinforcements: William H. T. Walker's Reserve Corps from Mississippi, and James Longstreet's corps from Virginia. Reinforced, Bragg used his augmented numbers to counterattack at Chickamauga. That victory came at heavy cost: 18,454 Rebels fell there. The Federals suffered nearly as badly, losing 16,351 men, and limped back to Chattanooga. Bragg's damaged force followed cautiously. Within days, both sides settled in for a siege.

William W. Mackall was Braxton Bragg's chief of staff, though he was no fan of his commander. Mackall, whose only field command came at Island No. 10 in 1862, was a close friend to Joseph Johnston. Mackall's letters to Johnston reveal much about the Army of Tennessee's internal workings. (loc)

Bragg's subordinates soon condemned him for wasting the fruits of victory by failing to pursue, even though at the time a successful pursuit was highly unlikely. Longstreet, new to the army, urged a Confederate turning movement very much in the spirit of Robert E. Lee—an offensive that would carry Bragg's force back into Middle Tennessee, isolating Rosecrans and forcing his surrender. Bragg rejected this plan for the very sound reason that the Army of Tennessee's logistics were wholly inadequate for such a move, something Longstreet was slow to grasp.

Bragg's reaction to his victory instead mirrored the Federal response to their defeat: to clean house. The Federals sent two corps commanders and a divisional commander packing, relieved of duty. For his part Bragg arrested Leonidas Polk and Thomas Hindman, charging them with failure to carry out orders. Despite the urging of his own chief of staff, Brig. Gen. William W. Mackall, to abstain from this vendetta, Bragg was unswayed. "If Bragg carries out his projects," noted Mackall gloomily in a private letter to his friend Joseph Johnston, "there will be great dissatisfaction. I have told him so, but he is hard to persuade when in prosperity, and I do not think my warning will be heeded until too late."

By October, that dissatisfaction had blossomed into full-fledged mutiny. Some of the army's officers began circulating a petition calling on President Davis to replace Bragg. This document, likely written by Maj. Gen. Simon B. Buckner, garnered the signatures of no less than twelve of Bragg's generals, including among them James Longstreet, D. H. Hill, and Patrick Cleburne. It grew out of a secret meeting held on October 4, where the gathered commanders somewhat disingenuously agreed to ask President Davis for Bragg's removal because "the condition of his health unfits him to command an army in the field." Mackall thought that "Longstreet has done more injury to the general [Bragg] than all the others put together."

Word of this turmoil soon spread. Despite his own low opinion of the army commander, Brig. Gen. St. John Liddell could not tolerate what he saw as "petty, miserable, political jealousies," and soon met with Bragg, hoping to persuade the army commander "of the propriety of making friends and quieting this dissatisfaction." To Liddell's "distress, *his* [Bragg's] mettle was also up, and beyond the control of dispassionate reason. . . . 'I want to get rid of all such generals [said Bragg.] . . . Let them send in their resignations. I shall accept every one without hesitation.'"

John C. Breckinridge, a former United States vice president, served as a corps commander under Bragg. Relations between the two men were not good. (loc)

President Davis, troubled both by the army's apparent inaction and Bragg's relief of Hindman and Polk, sent Brig. Gen. James Chesnut west as his special envoy. At Atlanta, Chesnut met with Polk, where he learned that the army's internal rot was more widespread than Davis supposed. "Your immediate presence in this army is urgently demanded," wired the alarmed envoy on October 5. In response, Davis set out, reaching Atlanta himself by the 8th.

Over the next week, Davis met with all the involved parties. Perhaps the most awkward moment for all concerned was the series of interviews Davis arranged between himself, the dissenters, and Bragg: each man was asked to air his grievances in Bragg's presence. Davis apparently believed that this would heal the breach between commander and commanded. He was dead wrong.

In the end, Davis sustained Bragg, who remained in command. The Confederate President did manage to convince Bragg to dismiss the charges against Hindman and Polk. Instead, Polk was given a command in Mississippi, allowing Lt. Gen. William

J. Hardee to return to the army in Polk's stead, replacing D. H. Hill, who would be sent home to North Carolina. For the time being, Hindman would continue his recuperative leave. Longstreet, Buckner, and the rest would remain. Then, believing he had reconciled the army's various dissatisfactions, Davis departed, first making a quick visit to Mississippi and then returning to Richmond.

Davis was badly out of touch. His visit solved nothing and left no one satisfied. As one example of how little Davis understood the turmoil within the army, he offered Bragg a new man, John C. Pemberton, who had disastrously surrendered Vicksburg that summer. Pemberton was universally despised across the south for that defeat, and no one wanted him in the Army of Tennessee. When St. John Liddell sarcastically asked fellow general Lucius Polk—a cousin of Leonidas Polk and a brigade commander in Cleburne's division—if Pemberton would replace Bragg, Polk reacted with dismay: "surely not him."

Thomas C. Hindman of Arkansas was one of the men Bragg relieved after Chickamauga. Davis dissuaded Bragg from pursuing any court-martial, but ill health prevented Hindman from returning to command until after Bragg himself was relieved. (loc)

If Bragg couldn't replace his disloyal commanders, he could still punish them through reorganization. He shuffled brigades and divisions around to create different power structures, trying to place the worst malcontents within the commands of the few men more amenable to Bragg's point of view. Major General Benjamin F. Cheatham's large, five-brigade Tennessee Division, for example, was broken up, with three brigades being transferred individually into divisions commanded by J. Patten Anderson, Alexander P. Stewart, and William H. T. Walker, each of whom was more favorably disposed toward the Army commander. Buckner was reduced from corps command to leading a division. He soon applied for—and was hastily granted—sick leave, traveling to Virginia. Only Longstreet's command, on loan as it was from Virginia, was beyond Bragg's reach; that command remained intact.

Davis's visit solved nothing. The bitter stew of discontent would continue to simmer, and the Federals would not be quiescent forever.

Brown's Ferry and Wauhatchie

CHAPTER FOUR

OCTOBER 24-30, 1863

October 24 dawned cold and misty. Generals Grant, Thomas, and Baldy Smith, as well as a sufficiency of staff officers, all departed Chattanooga, trotting across the bridge over the Tennessee River and onto Moccasin Bend. Smith led the party down to the river at Brown's Ferry where everyone dismounted and made his way to the water's edge. Due to the Tennessee's abrupt hairpin bend at the foot of Lookout Mountain, the river flowed north here for a considerable stretch—meaning that the line of hills and the notch marking the ferry landing lay due west of Grant's chosen observation point, but still, in a general sense, on the stream's southern bank. Rebel pickets stood on the opposite shore.

The river here was about 300 yards wide and free of rapids. A mile downstream, to the northwest, lay Williams Island, 320 acres of fertile farmland recently occupied by the 51st Ohio and 8th Kentucky Infantry, both belonging to Brig. Gen. Walter C. Whitaker's brigade of the IV Corps. Whitaker's remaining regiments picketed the riverbank along Moccasin Bend and occupied the range of hills crowding the bend's eastern side, planted there to support two batteries of Union artillery. Those guns were perfectly sited to interdict Confederate

This monument to the New York Regiments engaged at Wauhatchie sits alongside the modern Wauhatchie Pike, marking the site of the engagement. It is now in an industrial park. Lookout rises in the background. (hs)

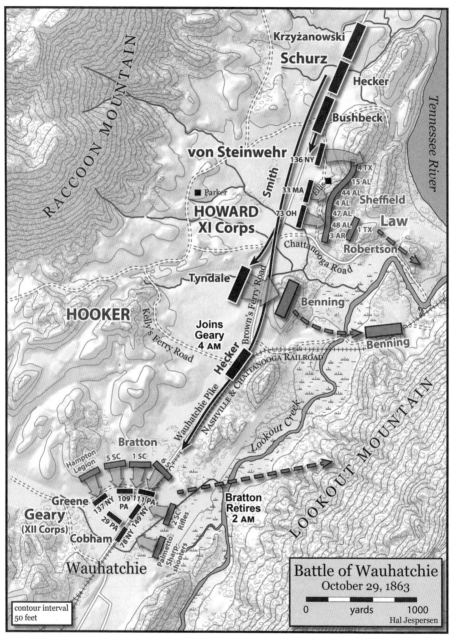

BATTLE OF WAUHATCHIE—A rare night action, the battle of Wauhatchie was one of the more confusing engagements of the war.

movements on the road over the shoulder of Lookout Mountain on the opposite bank. South Carolina Pvt. E. H. Acker of Hampton's Legion recalled that when his command was sent over the mountain to change pickets, "often in going and returning we would be shelled from what the boys called the Moccasin Battery . . . ." Sergeant Samuel H. Sprott of the 40th Alabama remembered that "the moving of troops had to take place under cover of darkness, and one can well imagine the difficulties attending such a movement."

The Rebels Grant observed belonged to Brig. Gen. Evander Law's brigade, a force of five Alabama regiments of Hood's division, Longstreet Corps. Only a portion of the brigade lined the bank here, in what locals called Lookout Valley, on the west side of Lookout Mountain's imposing mass. The Union artillery on Moccasin Bend made life so difficult for the Confederates that very few troops could be sustained in Lookout Valley for any length of time. Any supply wagons that attempted the shoulder road in daylight were soon driven back by a rain of Federal shells, and even night movements attracted enemy fire. As a result, the handful of Confederates stationed here were essentially semi-isolated from the rest of Bragg's army.

The Federal Road, now the walking path shown here, cut across Moccasin Bend to cross the Tennessee River here at Brown's Ferry. (hs)

From the riverbank, Grant noted "a picket station . . . of about twenty men," fully visible. These Rebels made no effort to pick off what appeared to them to be just another passel of curious Yankees admiring the view. "They did not fire upon us nor seem to be disturbed by our presence. They must have seen that we were all commissioned officers," mused the new commander, "but, I suppose, they looked upon the garrison of Chattanooga as prisoners of war."

Grant liked what he saw. Even at high water, the current was slow enough that a pontoon bridge could be thrown across the river easily. The line of hills on the far bank, if seized quickly, would form a defensive bulwark behind which the bridge could be completed without interference. It was time to disabuse Braxton Bragg and his army of their false sense of complacency.

The Federal plan was complex, with success hinging on careful timing. Departing Bridgeport, Maj. Gen. Joseph Hooker's corps was to pass Raccoon Mountain through Running Water Creek Gorge, enter Lookout Valley at the Wauhatchie rail junction, and then turn north towards Brown's Ferry. In the meantime—under Baldy Smith's overall direction—a hand-picked Union assault force led by Brig. Gen. William B. Hazen would quietly float down the Tennessee River under cover of darkness to land and quickly occupy the hills on both the left and right of Brown's Ferry.

Confederate Brig. Gen. Evander M. Law's Alabama Brigade picketed the banks of the Tennessee at Brown's Ferry, though Law himself was hopeful of being promoted to command John Bell Hood's division in the wake of Hood's wounding at Chickamauga. (b&l)

After Hazen's amphibious assault group was dug in atop the hills, Union engineers could then begin the work of assembling a pontoon bridge. Those engineers, the materials necessary for the bridging effort, and reinforcements for Hazen's command were all to have marched across Moccasin Bend during the night while Hazen's van was drifting downstream. Once the bridge was up, those additional troops would hurry across in case Hazen needed support and be ready to link up with Hooker's column. Once Hooker and Hazen connected, supplies could once more flow into Chattanooga unimpeded.

Hazen's expedition posed the most risk. The pontoon boats were rectangular barges, heavily laden and awkward to steer. The expedition would have to float downriver for nine miles in the dark, hugging the right bank to avoid detection, and landing at precisely the right spot just before dawn. Hazen, a gruff regular, wanted no volunteering. Instead the men tasked for this job should be hand-picked for their courage and judgment. "As each man was chosen," recalled Pvt. Philip Dines of the 41st Ohio, "he was also informed that his work for that night was of the most dangerous character—in fact, a forlorn hope. . . ." Even decades later, recalled Dines, "the reader will doubtless imagine [my] fright on receipt of this information." To further preserve secrecy, the men were not told all the details of their mission. They would carry nothing with them but weapons and ammunition. Bedrolls, haversacks, tin cups, and even bayonets were left behind, lest the clink of metal on metal give the Federals away.

Smith's amphibious movement was launched in the early morning hours of October 27; the plan was to have a defensible beachhead established and bridge construction well underway by shortly after sunup. Hooker's 11,000 men departed Bridgeport at sunrise that same morning. The two divisions of Maj. Gen. Oliver O. Howard's XI Corps led the march, followed by Brig. Gen. John W. Geary's division of the XII Corps. A handful of troopers from the Unionist 5th Tennessee and 1st Alabama Cavalries—some of them local men—led the way. Hooker's van marched as far as Running Water Creek that day, leaving some regiments to secure their rear. Confederate opposition amounted to no more than a handful of pickets who fell back at first contact. On October 28, Hooker intended to push on into Lookout Valley.

* * *

Confederate Brig. Gen. Micah Jenkins was Law's chief rival for Hood's command. With Law temporarily absent in late October, Jenkins weakened Law's brigade by ordering some of the regiments back over to the east side of Lookout Mountain. (loc)

Unwittingly, Confederate inattention greatly aided the Federal plan. The Army of Tennessee's internal conflicts were not solely the province of the senior commanders. Two Rebel brigadiers, Micah Jenkins and Evander M. Law, each commanded brigades in Hood's division. Law served in the division for more than a year and commanded it in action at both Gettysburg and Chickamauga after Hood was wounded. Jenkins was a recent transfer to the command from troops left behind in Virginia, a move Jenkins in part orchestrated to further his chances of promotion. Jenkins's date of rank made him senior to Law by two months, and with Hood still recovering, Jenkins assumed divisional command. Only rail delays prevented Jenkins from commanding the division at Chickamauga.

Law was no less ambitious. The key to permanent command of the division lay in securing promotion to major general, so both men mustered political influence to support their chances of securing that

In the postwar army, Union brigade commander William B. Hazen earned the sobriquet as "best-hated man in the army" due to his willingness to testify against corruption in the Grant administration. (loc)

promotion in the Confederate Congress. Their rivalry was not good natured.

In early October, James Longstreet dispatched Law to Lookout Valley, with the twin objectives of defending the riverbank and controlling the rail line from Bridgeport. Law noted that it would take a full division to adequately defend the valley, but Longstreet could only spare one brigade. Moreover, supplying even that size force in Lookout Valley would prove difficult; Law's men were nearly as short of rations as their putative "prisoners" penned up in Chattanooga.

Law disposed his small force carefully. Two regiments picketed the riverbank as far as Raccoon Mountain. Law held his other three regiments in reserve on the hills near the western foot of Lookout Mountain. Then, since everything seemed quiet, on October 25 Law took a short leave to go visit Hood down in Armuchee Valley, where the latter was recuperating, 30 miles to the southeast. That same day, General Jenkins ordered Law's three reserve regiments of Alabamans back to the eastern side of Lookout Mountain.

Jenkins's decision to shift the bulk of Law's brigade over to the east face of the mountain was never explained. Jenkins fell in battle the next spring and never had a chance to address the resultant postwar controversy. Law came to believe that it was a deliberate piece of sabotage, designed to damage his reputation by stripping his sector of the men needed to defend it at a critical moment. Deliberate malice seems unlikely, for while Jenkins might view Law as an unwelcome rival, Jenkins was also a Southern patriot, committed to the cause. More likely, it was a poorly timed effort by Jenkins to assert his authority over the division he now commanded and because the Confederates couldn't fully supply even five regiments on the far side of the Mountain. In any case, the Federals hadn't stirred in Lookout Valley for two weeks. Confederate attention lapsed.

* * *

Of course, Bragg and Longstreet remained at odds. Neither man had seen each other face to face since Davis departed the army; Bragg sat in his headquarters atop Missionary Ridge, studiously ignoring James Longstreet who, Achilles-like, sulked in his tent at the eastern foot of Lookout. On October 25, Bragg directed Longstreet to send a reconnaissance toward Bridgeport to determine if rumors of an imminent Federal crossing were true. Longstreet ignored the order. To be sure, Longstreet expected just such a crossing, but was convinced that instead of moving through Lookout Valley, Hooker's column would ascend Lookout Mountain somewhere south of Trenton, then turn north and attack his forces from the rear along the mountain's crest.

The boxlike pontoons, each loaded with Federals, floated noiselessly downstream until opposite the landing site, when bonfires from the Union side of the river lit up to mark the objective. (b&l)

The Federals were certainly stirring now, in the wee hours of October 27. Despite a couple of close calls, including one man falling overboard, Hazen's waterborne force remained undiscovered until the lead boats beached at Brown's Ferry. "At 4:30 in the morning," at General Smith's command, "Adjutant [Solomon] Homan of the First Ohio [Infantry] kindled the signal fires, as had been agreed upon." Shortly thereafter, the first Union boats appeared, quickly turning toward the far bank. Confederate pickets on duty at the ferry opened fire, but could do little to check this sudden onslaught. Major Albert Hart, Surgeon of the 41st Ohio, was in one of the leading pontoons. He'd been dozing when, suddenly, "[musket] balls [were] whizzing over and around . . . 'Push for the shore! Push for the shore!' . . . Our boats have dropped a little below our intended landing, but we reach the bank and leap ashore as we may."

Col. William C. Oates commanded the 15th Alabama, defending Brown's Ferry. Badly outnumbered and lacking any reinforcements, Oates nonetheless managed the best defense he could. He was wounded in the ensuing night action. (loc)

The Confederates belonged to Company B of Col. William C. Oates's 15th Alabama. Half of Oates's men were strung out along the riverbank, each picket-post consisting of three to five men, separated from the others by 150 to 200 yards. Oates and the remaining half of his command were camped a few hundred yards back from the water. The 4th Alabama lay farther downstream to Oates's left, beyond Williams Island.

Thanks to reports from the Rebel 9th Kentucky Cavalry, Oates already knew that two days prior a Union force (Hooker's) crossed the Tennessee at Bridgeport, headed for Lookout Valley. After forwarding that information over the mountain to Longstreet's headquarters, Oates awaited developments. When Company B's frantic report reached him, Oates quickly assembled his reserve—150 men—and counterattacked. It was so dark that Oates instructed each man "to place the muzzle of his rifle against the body of a Yankee when he fired." Despite this grim hyperbole, Oates's counterattack failed to regain the bank. After a short, confused firefight in which Oates himself fell wounded, the 15th retreated in disorder, abandoning their camps to the enemy. The 4th Alabama fell back once they received word of the unfolding disaster.

Union battalions scrambled up the hills flanking the ferry site and began to dig in. Within ten minutes of landing, marveled Surgeon Hart, men of the 23rd Kentucky "were already cutting down trees to build a breastwork." As each boat was unloaded, it was paddled back across the river, either to ferry across more troops or to become part of the new bridge. Within a short time, the Federal lodgment was secure. The operation had been a complete success.

* * *

That next morning Bragg rode over to consult with Longstreet. Both men ascended the mountain. Bragg was furious that Lookout Valley had fallen so easily. Longstreet was no less angry, and doubtless chagrinned at his failure to anticipate the Brown's Ferry movement. Bragg wanted Longstreet to attack, but, as Longstreet now pointed out, the bridgehead was now both heavily fortified and largely reinforced. While they were meeting, Confederate signalers on Lookout's west brow sent word of yet another Union column pushing out of Running Water Canyon and to the junction at Wauhatchie, then turning north towards Brown's Ferry. The generals hurried to look for themselves.

These were Hooker's men, completing their march from Bridgeport. They moved in two bodies. First came the XI Corps, which made junction with the Army of the Cumberland force before stopping. Then, at some distance behind, John Geary's small division of the XII Corps, accompanying a large supply train, halted and went into camp at Wauhatchie three miles short of Brown's Ferry. James Longstreet sensed an opportunity.

John White Geary was a pre-war politician, serving as both the first mayor of San Francisco and as territorial governor of troubled Kansas in the 1850s. (loc)

Detachments reduced Geary's division to a mere six regiments and a battery, numbering only 1,600 men, his relative weakness clearly visible to observers at the mountain. Longstreet proposed a night attack, sending a substantial force down into Lookout Valley to crush this impudent column of Yankees at Wauhatchie. Wanting to strike a major blow, Bragg suggested the use of Longstreet's whole corps, as well as offering up a division of Breckinridge's corps if needed.

This idea of a larger assault never materialized, though the reasons are unclear. Bragg also expected Longstreet to assault the Brown's Ferry bridgehead, either after or in conjunction with the strike at Geary. Longstreet felt that the larger Union position was too strong to seize in a *coup de main*, and focused his attention on Wauhatchie. In his memoirs, Longstreet indicated that he intended to use Jenkins's and McLaws's divisions—in all, about 10,000 men—for the blow. However, McLaws either never received his orders or (so Longstreet assumed) they were countermanded by Bragg, leaving only Jenkins's four brigades to make the attack.

Whatever the cause for McLaws's non-participation, it was probably a fortunate blunder. The logistics of moving that many men into Lookout Valley over the course of a single night were unworkable, while supporting them through the ensuing days until a sufficient force was assembled would be equally impossible. Besides, a drawn-out movement would only tip the Rebel hand. A quick strike, preserving the element of surprise, was the only option likely to have any chance of success, and that meant using no more than a single division.

Jenkins's execution of what remained of the mission, however, was equally flawed. Major James L. Coker of the 6th South Carolina, sent to conduct a personal reconnaissance of this movement, reported back to Jenkins's headquarters at sunset. "After receiving my report," noted Coker, "[Jenkins] seemed disturbed." Coker's intelligence suggested that "a heavy body of infantry, with artillery," guarded the Union wagon train. According to Coker's recollection, "Jenkins went to General Longstreet with my report, but it made no impression there, and the plan as originally made was insisted upon."

Of his four available brigades, Jenkins sent only his own South Carolina command, now led by Col. James Bratton, to attack Wauhatchie. Two brigades, under Law, were assigned the task of blocking the Brown's Ferry Road and preventing Howard's XI Corps from reinforcing Geary. Finally, Henry Benning's brigade guarded the crossing over Lookout Creek, to ensure a safe retreat path should it be needed. The movement took longer than expected, but shortly after midnight Bratton's 1,800 men brushed aside Geary's pickets to assail his encamped force.

The resulting combat was that rarest of Civil War engagements: a deliberately planned night fight. Geary, who expected to be attacked, was as prepared as he could be, with pickets well out. Geary was not pleased with his circumstances, detached from Hooker's main body; only Hooker seemed unconcerned. That afternoon, General

Hazen, alarmed at Hooker's nonchalance, had urged Hooker to place his entire force in "a compact line across the valley. . . . But being confident that the enemy would not disturb him, Hooker refused to change his dispositions."

Geary's position centered on a small knoll just west of the rail junction, upon which Geary stationed Capt. Charles Atwell's Battery E of the Pennsylvania Light Artillery. Also serving in Atwell's battery was the general's son, Lt. Edward R. Geary, as second in command. General Geary stationed battalions of the 29th Pennsylvania infantry at various points of the compass some distance from his camp, as pickets. The remaining five regiments formed a loose defensive box, oriented mostly eastward, facing the mountain.

Bratton's first clash came when his van—six companies of the 6th South Carolina, in skirmish order—clashed with companies C and G of the 29th. First came a challenge, then a lone shot by a Federal, and then, recalled Pvt. David Mouat of the 29th, "a volley was immediately fired by the [unknown] command in front." The Federals realized Confederates badly outnumbered them. "'For God's sake Dave come on, the woods are full of Rebs,'" urged one of Mouat's comrades, and with that, the two blue companies "ran down the slope towards the railroad."

The 29th had done well, alerting Geary to the fact that the enemy was approaching from the north; quickly, the small force re-oriented so that the 109th and 111th Pennsylvania faced in that direction, supported by Atwell's four cannon. The 137th and 149th New York were still moving up to prolong the Union left, adjacent to the 109th, when the South Carolinians struck.

With the Union pickets swept away, Bratton pushed three regiments south. The 2nd South Carolina Rifles anchored the Rebel left, aligned along the Nashville & Chattanooga tracks, with the 1st and 5th regiments extending the Confederate line westward. Colonel George A. Cobham, commanding Geary's 2nd Brigade, was with the

Col. John Bratton commanded Jenkins's South Carolina brigade during the Wauhatchie fight. He was a pre-war medical doctor and successful planter. (loc)

111th, anchoring Geary's apex just in front of the knoll. "I could hear them advancing," recorded Cobham, "and ordered the men to lie down. As soon as the advancing lines . . . could be seen through the darkness I ordered the men to fire. This was something they did not expect, as they supposed us all to be asleep."

Cobham's observation was apparently correct. The 2nd Rifles halted and then fell back in some disorder. This retreat halted the 1st and 5th, in turn, but instead of also retiring they returned fire, their rounds striking the 137th, just finishing its re-alignment, and the 149th, still hurrying into position. The 137th held, but the 149th had worse luck. The livestock from some of the division's ammunition and ambulance wagons stampeded at the sudden fire, tearing through the 149th's ranks.

Despite believing that he was badly outnumbered, Bratton reinforced the 2nd Rifles with the 6th South Carolina, and now attempted a double envelopment, sending the Hampton Legion to the 5th's right with orders to flank the Federals from the west, while the Palmetto Sharpshooters shifted leftward across the tracks to duplicate this feat from the east.

Gen. Geary's eighteen-year-old son Edward, a member of Knap's Pennsylvania Battery, was killed during the engagement. Edward's promotion to captain had just been approved and was in the general's pocket when Edward expired in his father's arms. (loc)

It almost worked. But the Legion could not rout the 137th: Regimental Adjutant James E. Mix refused the two left-most companies ninety degrees, which blunted the Legion's advance. Nor could the Palmettos turn the Union right. The 149th, now rallied, rushed into line along the railroad embankment, facing east, with the 78th New York coming into line alongside them. Both sides settled into a static fire, burning through the ammunition in their cartridge boxes.

The Union artillery—Knap's Pennsylvania Battery—bore the worst of this fire. Silhouetted on the knoll with each gun flash, Rebel fire decimated the gunners. Captain Atwell fell, wounded; then Lieutenant Geary, killed. Brigade commander George Greene was also wounded, elevating the 137th's highly competent colonel, David Ireland, to the job.

Colonel Martin Gary, commanding the Hampton Legion, still thought he saw a chance to smash the Federals. The Legion had already overrun part of the Union camp, where the Rebels captured a set of Union colors. Now, Gary thought, "I could have charged the battery with every indication of success, but I had advanced so fast that I had not communicated with Colonel Coward [commanding the 5th South Carolina], and already I was within range of fire. I sent a courier to notify [Colonel Coward] of my position and the advantage I had gained, but before he could return I received [an] order to withdraw my regiment."

That order came from Bratton. The time was near 3:00 a.m. Fighting had been raging for perhaps two hours. Bratton was preparing to order a final effort when he received alarming news: Law's two brigades had been attacked and were falling back. If Bratton did not immediately follow suit, his whole command would be cut off.

Smith and Tyndale Hills

CHAPTER FIVE

OCTOBER 29-30, 1863

At 1:00 a.m., Joe Hooker, whose indifference to the exposed nature of Geary's division had placed that command into peril in the first place, awoke to "the mutterings of a heavy musketry" coming from the south. Grasping that Geary had been attacked, Hooker quickly sent an order to General Howard to reinforce Geary with the "nearest division," led by Carl Schurz, followed by the rest of the XI Corps. Not satisfied, Hooker also sent two aides directly to Schurz, instructing him to move to join Geary. Then, a few minutes later, Hooker summoned Schurz to his headquarters tent to repeat those orders in person. Schurz complied while his troops formed up.

Law's two brigades were supposed to prevent exactly this occurrence, deploying so as to block the road running from Brown's Ferry to the rail junction. Instead of arranging his force physically astride that road, however, Law chose to occupy a line of hills paralleling it to the east. Only a line of Confederate skirmishers pushed forward to interdict the actual road. In daylight, this might have been sufficient to keep the XI Corps from sweeping past his position and striking Bratton's rear. Darkness changed the equation.

This monument to the 10 New York regiments in Von Steinwehr's and Schurz's divisions of the XI Corps marks their advance on Smith's Hill. Text on three sides of the monument describes the action of the regiments. (ew)

Law held no enthusiasm for his mission. Conferring with Jenkins just before night fell, Law opined that "one division was insufficient . . . [and] that a failure would be the result, and the troops engaged . . . would be seriously injured." Jenkins could only reply that he "had positive orders to proceed."

Law's brigade moved out at 7:00 p.m., crossing Lookout Creek perhaps an hour later, and deployed in an open field just west of one of the "hogback" hills that lined the bank of the Tennessee south of Brown's Ferry. They then moved up to the crest of the hill and, finding it unoccupied, began to entrench. Brigadier General Jerome Robertson's Texas Brigade came up in support. Sometime later, however, Law made an unfortunate discovery: he was on the wrong hill.

As Law's skirmishers pushed forward to the Brown's Ferry Road, they crossed over another "hogback" directly to their front, which overlooked the road. They also captured Union skirmishers— XI Corps men who confirmed to Law that there was indeed a sizeable Federal force in the valley, stronger than his own. Nevertheless, the next hill was also unoccupied, so Law moved his brigade forward. While he did so, Bratton's and Brig. Gen. Henry Benning's brigades finished crossing Lookout Creek—Benning occupying yet another hill on Law's right, ordered to block the road, and Bratton turning south to strike Geary.

It was the noise of Bratton's attack that so excited Hooker, who certainly had been warned of Geary's exposure and knew full well that if his command were overwhelmed at Wauhatchie, Joe Hooker would rightly bear the blame. Unfortunately, however, Hooker's frantic burst of activity, aimed at getting the XI Corps moving as soon as possible, was working at cross-purposes.

Schurz's men fell into ranks under "bright moonlight." Hooker's initial orders instructed Schurz to immediately dispatch one brigade southward to occupy "the hill in the angle formed by" the Wauhatchie Road and the railroad—the very same hill supposed to be occupied by Benning's

Georgians. Schurz would later report that his lead brigade, commanded by Brig. Gen. Hector Tyndale, moved down the road, and after colliding with Confederate pickets, "speedily dislodged" Benning's Confederates. In fact, Tyndale's brigade encountered only those enemy skirmishers.

By the time Tyndale reached what would thereafter be called Tyndale's Hill, virtually all of Benning's troops were gone. Soon after reaching the crest, Benning discovered he was too far from the road he was supposed to interdict, so he advanced. Shortly thereafter, Jenkins ordered him to move

The small housing development in the foreground is where Bratton's South Carolinians advanced, moving from left to right. The slope in the left of the frame is Tyndale Hill. In the background, Lookout towers above all. (hs)

his four Georgia regiments several hundred yards south to the railroad, from where he could better protect the bridges leading back over Lookout Creek and—for the Rebels—safety. With unknown numbers of Federals stirring off to the north, Jenkins was already thinking of calling the whole operation off.

The Federals were no less subject to the confusion and uncertainty of a night engagement. While moving south, Schurz reported that his column received "a full volley" from a "rebel [Law's brigade] force concealed in the woods . . . on my left." Other skirmishers appeared to be blocking the road. In order to bypass this unknown degree of resistance and to take what he thought was a short cut to save time, Schurz directed his men into an open field to his right, which turned out to be a swamp. This detour and yet more skirmishing with unknown numbers of the enemy ate up considerable time, all while Geary's drama played out to the south.

Next came Brig. Gen. Adolph von Steinwehr's division of two brigades, Col. Orland Smith's brigade in the lead. Again Law's men opened fire,

Maj. Gen. Carl Schurz was among the most well known of the German refugees that fled the 1848 revolution. Though he lacked military training, Schurz's respect within the German community made him an obvious choice for political generalship. He proved competent, if not gifted, in the job of command. (loc)

disrupting the 73rd Ohio. Smith halted and formed line facing east at the base of what would be called Smith's Hill, awaiting further orders. Major Charles Howard, aide to his brother the general, arrived to confer. Howard urged an attack to take the hill. Hooker, not far off at the Ellis House, concurred, directing Steinwehr to have Smith assault the hill directly and place his other brigade in support.

Dutifully the 450 men of the Union 73rd Ohio and 33rd Massachusetts charged up the hill. They were attacking roughly three times their number, Law's five Alabama regiments as well as Arkansans and Texans—half of Robertson's brigade—all behind hasty entrenchments. The Federals groped their way up the slope, blundering into those defenses at close range, only to be hammered by enemy volleys and forced back.

Smith organized a second effort, adding in the 136th New York to try to work around the north end of Smith Hill in an effort to outflank the enemy. But coordinating movements in the dark was difficult, and both the 33rd and 73rd were again thrown back in confusion.

Still, the New Yorkers' flanking effort had an effect. Colonel James L. Sheffield was commanding Law's brigade, since Law was at the time in charge of both his own and Robertson's commands, and when word from some Texans reached Sheffield that Union troops were working their way around the northern shoulder of the hill, threatening his rear, Sheffield pulled two companies out of the center of his line to reinforce his right, opening up a 30 yard gap between the 15th and 44th Alabama. Some Massachusetts men clambered over the breastworks at that gap to take the 44th in flank, which forced those Alabamans into a disordered retreat, leaving an even bigger gap. The 44th rallied and reestablished a new line, partly with the help of Col. Alexander Lowther of the 15th, who left his own regiment to help rally the 44th; but then the 15th, witnessing the 44th's break, also fell back. Suddenly, Law was faced with a crisis atop Smith Hill.

Sheffield's decision to shift the two companies was probably unnecessary since Law had already brought up the 4th Texas—the third of Robertson's four regiments—to reinforce the point threatened by the 136th New York, but other factors were now weighing on Law. After the first Union charge was repulsed, he received word from Jenkins that Bratton had met a strong force and was falling back. Law was to hold until the South Carolinians were extricated from danger. But Law also knew, based on General Robertson's observations, that he did not have enough troops to hold Smith Hill and effectively cover the space between that hill and the Tennessee River, where another road ran behind Law's right. Some Federals (the 136th New York) were already threatening in that direction, and if more appeared, it might be Law who was cut off.

Accordingly, Law ordered a retreat, which Sheffield began just as the 33rd and 73rd renewed their charge. The two Federal regiments struck just as the Alabamians were moving out, triggering a panic. Alabama private William Jordan of the 15th later recalled that "[we] retreated in great confusion, some of the officers lost their swords, some lost their hats, etc." Fellow Alabamian Mitchell Houghton admitted that some of the 15th simply "stampeded to the rear." A number of Alabamians were captured here. That stampede triggered a similar fright in the 4th Texas, who were now in danger of being cut off in turn. The Texans broke for the bridge over Lookout Creek, "hallooing 'routed, routed'" as they went.

It was a surprising feat. Two small regiments from the much-maligned XI Corps—famously mocked as the "flying Dutchmen" of Chancellorsville and Gettysburg—launched a frontal attack against the better part of two brigades of the Confederate army's finest, both behind breastworks, driving the Rebels off in considerable disorder.

Fortunately for the Confederates, Federal confusion precluded any real threat of Jenkins's command being destroyed. The fight for Smith Hill focused Union attention away from rescuing

Adolph Von Steinwehr, a German from Brunswick, was not a revolutionary. He served as a junior officer before emigrating to the United States in 1847. He returned to Brunswick in 1849, married, and then came back to America in 1854. (loc)

Brig. Gen. Henry L. Benning commanded the Georgians that for a time defended Tyndale Hill. Benning was a pre-war judge, an associate justice on the Georgia Supreme Court, and noted fire-eating Secessionist. (loc)

Col. Samuel H. Hurst led the 73rd Ohio in storming Smith's Hill against Law's brigade. Hurst was a pre-war school teacher and self-taught lawyer. He took to soldiering well. (loc)

Geary, so much so that at one point, as Hooker took personal direction of the action, General Howard volunteered to press on to Wauhatchie with nothing more than his cavalry escort. This high-ranking reconnaissance never came to pass, but Howard seemed to make no other contributions to the battle. Schurz's remaining two brigades halted at the Chattanooga-Wauhatchie crossroads, free of the swamp but now mired in confusion. Colonel Wladamir Krzyzanowski's brigade stopped first as the Polish-born officer waited for someone to tell him what to do. Colonel Freidrich Hecker ordered his men to bull their way through Krzyzanowski's ranks to press on, only to be halted by Schurz a short while later.

Hooker and Schurz would later quarrel about that halt, with Hooker later questioning both Schurz's and Hecker's "courage and valor" and suggesting that Schurz flagrantly disobeyed the order to reach Geary. Schurz took umbrage, pointing out conflicting orders issued to him by Howard and then Hooker himself. The matter was resolved when Schurz was granted a court of inquiry in February 1864, which absolved both himself and Hecker of any wrongdoing.

It would be another two hours before things were sorted out on site. Hecker's brigade finally reached Geary's position just before dawn, around 5:00 a.m. By then, all the Confederates were gone.

The Wauhatchie fight produced dissatisfaction on both sides. While Geary's men fought well, Geary was profoundly distressed over the loss of his son, which only magnified his anger toward Hooker concerning the decision to leave Geary's command alone and exposed at Wauhatchie. Tension between Hooker and the XI Corps officers also did not abate. Eventually, when the XI and XII Corps were consolidated under Hooker's permanent direction, both Howard and Schurz were transferred to other commands.

On the Confederate side, that dissatisfaction penetrated to the highest levels of army command. In addition to the ongoing conflict between Jenkins and Law, Bragg's and Longstreet's mutual disdain now hardened into a permanent enmity. Despite the resultant diminishing of his manpower, Bragg judged his army to be better off without James Longstreet's presence, and would seek to be rid of him soon.

Interlude

CHAPTER SIX

NOVEMBER 1-20, 1863

As October closed, Ulysses S. Grant had reason to be satisfied. The Army of the Cumberland was now restored to full rations, and could even begin to accumulate a surplus for future operations. The first of the promised reinforcements—Hooker's column—had joined the army, and more were on the way.

In the first days of November, Grant undertook another comprehensive survey of his command, riding the picket lines, minutely inspecting each aspect of the Federal position. He had no intention of resting on laurels already won. With Bragg still clinging to Lookout Mountain and Missionary Ridge, Grant intended to strike soon.

In his memoirs, Grant related an amusing anecdote: an encounter with Confederate pickets near the mouth of Chattanooga Creek, where fraternization occurred daily. At one place, where a fallen tree spanned the creek and was used by both sides to draw water, Grant saw "a soldier dressed in blue on this log, I rode up to him, commenced conversing with him, and asked whose corps he belonged to. He was very polite, and touching his hat to me, said he belonged to General Longstreet's corps. I asked him a few questions—but not with a

These rifled cannon sit atop Lookout Mountain, in theory well placed to shell Union positions in Chattanooga and on Moccasin Bend. In reality, the extreme range and defective Confederate ammunition—mainly fuses—rendered them ineffective. (em)

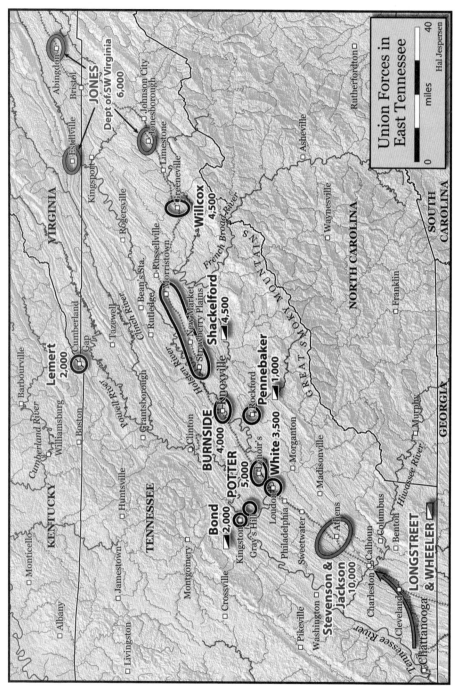

UNION FORCES IN EAST TENNESSEE—Though Ambrose Burnside commanded considerable forces in East Tennessee, amounting to some 26,500 men, his troops were considerably scattered, deployed to secure territory and block raids rather than face a full-scale invasion by the Rebels.

view of gaining any particular information—all of which he answered, and I rode off."

Grant's confusion was easily explained. Just prior to coming west, Longstreet's men were issued new uniforms of dark "steel gray" British wool. Western troops—both Federal and Confederate— often mistook the new arrivals for Union men.

James Longstreet's corps was not destined to remain at Chattanooga much longer. On November 3, perhaps while Grant and his new acquaintance were chatting, Bragg conferred with Longstreet, William Hardee—newly arrived from Alabama to replace D. H. Hill—and other senior officers. Union control of Lookout Valley rendered any Rebel siege moot. Accordingly, Longstreet proffered a new plan: to cross the Tennessee River near Bridgeport and strike directly at the Union railhead, ideally doing so before the Federals could be further reinforced.

Once again the plan foundered on logistics. Bragg's supply system couldn't maintain a sufficient force in Lookout Valley, let alone support all or most of the army in a move against Bridgeport. The proposal was cursorily dismissed. Longstreet didn't even mention it in his memoirs. Instead, talk turned to East Tennessee.

President Jefferson Davis and Gen. Robert E. Lee never intended Longstreet's transfer to be permanent. Longstreet's troops contributed to Bragg's great victory. Now it was time to think about returning them to Virginia, where they would be badly needed. Davis suggested as much on October 29: "It has occurred to me," he wired, "that if the operations on your left should be delayed . . . that you might advantageously assign Longstreet . . . the task of expelling Burnside [in East Tennessee] and thus place him in position, according to circumstances, to hasten or delay his return to the army of General Lee."

This idea appealed to Bragg on two levels. If a Rebel army could clear East Tennessee, the rail line through Knoxville could be returned to Confederate control, restoring direct communications with Richmond. Moreover, a Rebel army at Knoxville

By early November, James Longstreet was eager to be quit of Braxton Bragg—who was no less eager to see the last of Longstreet. (dp)

could threaten Grant's own flank at Chattanooga, or even pose a threat to Union control of Middle Tennessee. And by specifically sending Longstreet, Bragg could also rid himself of what had become yet another troublesome subordinate—the only remaining hard-core anti-Bragg conspirator who so far had not been relieved, transferred, or demoted.

For his part, Longstreet liked the idea both for its strategic possibilities as well as the chance to get out from under a vexing superior. But any attack into East Tennessee could only succeed if the Confederates struck quickly, with overwhelming force.

It is a dictum of military strategy that an inferior force, using interior lines, can fight and defeat a larger opponent by attacking scattered elements of that opponent's army before those elements united: the classic definition of "defeat in detail." This was the situation Bragg now faced. When combined, Grant's force would outnumber him greatly. As of early November, however, Thomas had only 40,000 men in Chattanooga. Hooker had roughly 15,000 in Lookout Valley. Sherman was approaching from Mississippi with another 25,000, but they would be several weeks in arriving. Burnside also numbered 25,000, but his troops were scattered through East Tennessee; given time enough he could perhaps detach 15,000 men to menace Bragg's right flank. Grant would eventually mass 90,000 or 100,000 men at the decisive point. Bragg's total force numbered about 60,000. The only way to shorten those odds was to strike first.

Bragg already had 10,000 infantry in East Tennessee, two divisions under command of Maj. Gen. Carter L. Stevenson, supported by 5,000 cavalry. Longstreet advocated taking his own 11,000 men to join Stevenson and quickly capture Knoxville. This was a reasonable plan. Of Burnside's 25,000 Federals, only 8,000 faced Stevenson, with a few thousand more holding Knoxville. Another 6,000 opposed the Rebels in Virginia and 3,000 were stationed at Cumberland Gap. Burnside's force was clearly vulnerable to piecemeal destruction.

The plan was risky. To compensate, Longstreet suggested that Bragg fall back somewhere behind the "Chickamauga River." Doing so would shorten Bragg's lines, and extend Grant's own position. Militarily, it was a sound proposal. Politically, abandoning the siege of Chattanooga implied failure. While no one discussed the political ramifications of such a move, they were almost certainly on Bragg's mind. Bragg decided that Longstreet must go to East Tennessee, but Bragg was not going to fall back on Ringgold, or even give up Lookout Mountain.

Like Hooker, Ambrose Burnside was another former commander of the Army of the Potomac who had come up short in the Lincoln Administration's estimation. Burnside had performed better in secondary theaters, most notably North Carolina early in the war, and now in East Tennessee. (loc)

Due both to the Army of Tennessee's serious logistical shortcomings and the continued infighting among its generals, the Confederate lunge toward Knoxville was neither swift nor strong. Instead of combining Longstreet and Stevenson, Bragg simply replaced Stevenson's men with Longstreet's. Instead of favorable odds, Longstreet would have to settle for parity. The movement also took far longer than expected. Longstreet lacked an adequate supply train, good guides who knew East Tennessee, an effective pontoon train, or even a quartermaster department that could find supplies to feed his men once in East Tennessee.

The railroad, upon which Longstreet depended for the first 50 miles of his move, was also completely inadequate, with locomotives so underpowered that the troops had to dismount and walk alongside when going uphill. It would take Longstreet a week to shift his troops via the rails, leaving him to complain that his men could have marched the distance in "half the time." Scrounging sufficient livestock and wagons to support his advance beyond the railhead took even longer.

By November 6, Longstreet's men were on their way, with Stevenson's command trickling back to replace them. The slowness of this troop swap created a Confederate window of vulnerability that did not go unnoticed. That day, Union signalers reported that the "Rebel camps at [the] foot of Lookout on [the] east side appear to be broken up, as not a dozen tents are to be seen, and very

few men." Confederate deserters confirmed that Longstreet's corps was leaving, with only "Bragg's old army" left in front of Chattanooga. This news seemed to confirm Burnside's own report: "the enemy are making formidable demonstration in the eastern part of the state."

Grant reacted quickly. On November 7, he ordered George Thomas to launch "an attack on the northern end of Missionary Ridge, with all the force you can bring to bear against it, and, when that is carried, to threaten, and even attack, if possible, the enemy's line of communications [the railroad] between Dalton and Cleveland." If Thomas's artillery crews lacked sufficient horses to draw the guns, Grant continued, "Mules must be taken from the . . . ambulances, or . . . officers dismounted and their horses taken." Finally, "the movement should not be made one moment later than to-morrow morning."

That blow never landed. Thomas, whose character was in many ways the exact opposite of Grant's, felt the Army of the Cumberland was in no condition to move. Thomas was by nature a meticulous, careful planner. He knew the army's condition far better than did Grant: all the army's livestock were in dreadful shape, with thousands of army horses either starving or already dead of malnutrition. The teams drawing ambulances and the officers' mounts were in no better shape than the artillery teams. Why Grant thought

Lt. Henry Kircher of the 12th Missouri Infantry toiled with Sherman. Though born in Illinois, Kircher's family was German, and he closely identified with the German-American community. A machinist by trade, he enlisted first in the 9th Illinois, later accepting a commission in the 12th. (alpl)

Confederate Gen. William J. Hardee was no stranger to the Army of Tennessee, though he had transferred to Mississippi before Chickamauga. Now he was back, replacing D. H. Hill. (loc)

Benjamin F. Cheatham had his failings as a commander, but his troops admired him nonetheless. Bragg had disliked him since Stones River, where Cheatham was reputed to be dead-drunk. (b&l)

otherwise remains unknown. The fact is, however, if the Army of the Cumberland did indeed move on November 8, it would do so without artillery, baggage, or ordnance wagons, and with most officers already afoot. Grant's proposed blow would be more of a feeble tap. The army was simply not ready for an offensive.

Nonetheless, Grant chafed. In his memoirs, he chided Thomas for "persist[ing] in the declaration that he could not move a single piece of artillery, and could not see how he could possibly comply with the order." Ultimately Grant acquiesced, but he would not forget Thomas's apparent recalcitrance.

In fact, the delay worked to Union advantage. Burnside confidently pointed out that as he fell back toward Knoxville, he would draw Longstreet's men farther away from Bragg, making it that much harder for one to reinforce the other. As Longstreet's men boarded the cars bound for East Tennessee, they were taking permanent leave of the Army of Tennessee to embark on a journey—however long and bitter—

William Henry Talbot Walker's nickname was "Shotpouch," acquired due to his tendency to collect enemy lead. He was that rare breed: a Bragg supporter in the ranks of the Army of Tennessee's generals. (b&l)

that would return them to Robert E. Lee and the Army of Northern Virginia.

Bragg has been heavily criticized for sending Longstreet away, even though the idea originated with President Davis. Bragg, however, did little to realistically support the movement or try to ensure success. Ultimately, it may be that Bragg's only objective in sending Longstreet away was to rid himself of a troublemaker. As Bragg confided to one of his divisional commanders, Brig. Gen. St. John Liddell, his goal was "to get rid of [Longstreet] and see what he could accomplish on his own resources."

* * *

The next fortnight saw a lull. Grant chose to wait for the arrival of Gen. William T. Sherman's expeditionary force, drawn from Mississippi. Sherman's column included three divisions of the XV Army Corps led by Maj. Gen. Frank P. Blair and a division of the VXII Corps under Brig. Gen. John E. Smith. These were the troops with whom Grant had conquered Vicksburg; he trusted them implicitly. Moreover, Sherman was his reliable subordinate, the man who could be counted on to execute an order promptly, without baulking.

But Sherman was still toiling his way across Northern Alabama. Originally ordered to rebuild the Memphis & Ohio railroad as he came, Sherman was still at Iuka, Mississippi, on October 27, when Grant's instruction to forgo the repairs and press on to Chattanooga as quickly as could be managed reached him. Thereafter, he made better time, but it was still a grueling march. Not until November 4 did Sherman's column cross the Tennessee River in northwest Alabama, ready to press onward.

In a letter home, Capt. Henry Kircher of the 12th Missouri infantry detailed his command's itinerary for much of November: "On average, we went 15-16 miles a day: in all, close to 200 miles in 14 days." Along the way, Kircher witnessed much desolation, especially in Alabama, and complained—as men in the ranks are ever wont to do—about that which he found incomprehensible. "By the way, without any sense or reason, we took the longest and the worst route. Just look on the map. We went in a zigzag." At least Kircher and his colleagues were spared combat, for "on the whole march we didn't see a single enemy." By November 18, the 12th Missouri reached Bridgeport, bringing up the rear of Sherman's column.

There was actually good reason for the "zigzag." Sherman needed to find a place where his army could ford the Elk River, swollen by October's rains. Crossing the Elk lower down, near where it flowed into the Tennessee, would require bridging or steamboats serving as ferries—a much slower operation. In this case, longer marches meant shorter delays.

At Bridgeport, "nobody knows what is to become of us," Kircher confessed. "I can just tell you this much; that we are going across the Tennessee . . . tomorrow or the next day, where the . . . 15th A. Corps [is] already assembled. . . . All the time you hear first this then that, and then both of those are again tossed into a cocked hat by a third story. However," he concluded, "I do believe this much; that the next 14 days will bring us a great step nearer to the end of the war."

Though the march across Alabama produced little action, one loss of a more personal nature haunted Sherman. His nine-year-old son, Willie, died of dysentery and malaria in a Memphis hotel room on October 3. The boy became infected while the children were visiting their father at Vicksburg. Willie was his father's clear favorite of the six, "the one I most prised [sic] on earth." Sherman blamed himself. Blanketed with grief, his focus was not always on duty.

* * *

While Sherman toiled and grieved, Bragg fiddled. With Longstreet gone, the Confederate commander embarked on a major reorganization of his army, the latest of many that fall.

Patrick R. Cleburne was probably Bragg's best divisional commander. Born in Ireland, he settled in Helena, Arkansas, as a druggist before the war. His only military training was as a corporal with the British army in the 1840s. (b&l)

Back in July, the Army of Tennessee had consisted of two infantry corps (with a total of five divisions), one cavalry corps (of two divisions), and an independent cavalry division (Forrest's.) As reinforcements swelled Bragg's ranks, the army grew to contain eleven infantry divisions organized into five corps and four cavalry divisions in two mounted corps. Seven separate corps was tantamount to command chaos, too much for one man to manage. Bragg applied a temporary fix on the battlefield of Chickamauga when he created two wing commands, assigning them to Leonidas Polk and James Longstreet.

Now, every one of those corps commanders were gone: relieved, demoted, or simply sent away. In order to streamline his chain of command, Bragg reverted to a two-corps structure, each with four infantry divisions, plus all the cavalry concentrated into a single corps under Maj. Gen. Joseph Wheeler. William J. Hardee commanded one infantry corps, John C. Breckinridge the other. Breckinridge's position was temporary, while Maj. Gen. Thomas C. Hindman recuperated from his Chickamauga wound. This absence suited Bragg, for while Breckinridge was no favorite, Hindman was one of the officers Bragg had intended to court-martial until dissuaded by President Davis.

Nor was Bragg content to stop there. The army commander transferred brigades and even regiments between formations to suit his purposes. Some of these transfers were designed to bring together troops from the same state, but others were designed specifically to break up perceived anti-Bragg power blocks within the army.

One such re-organization dismantled Maj. Gen. Benjamin F. Cheatham's large five-brigade division of nearly all Tennessee troops. Bragg's popularity among the Tennesseans had waned since he abandoned Middle Tennessee without a fight; now Bragg saw them as troublemakers. Cheatham's command was reduced to four brigades, only two of which had previously served with him; two other brigades of Alabamans and

Mississippians, their commanders untainted by disaffection, were transferred in. Cheatham's other three brigades were each transferred to a different division, commanded by perceived Bragg loyalists: Maj. Gen. William H. T. Walker, Brig. Gen. Patton Anderson, and Maj. Gen. Alexander P. Stewart.

Cheatham's division's dismemberment revealed how distracted Bragg had become by the army's internal turmoil. The Tennessee division had served as a unit for more than a year, fighting well in several actions. They were a proven combat organization. Breaking them up was a blow to their morale.

Further blows were afoot. That month Bragg's inadequate commissary was forced to cut rations. On November 15, the daily meat ration was reduced by one fourth to "three-quarters of a pound of fresh meat" per man per day, with extra rice and sugar as substitutes. The army also suffered from a paucity of fresh vegetables. Though not widely understood at the time, this lack meant that the average soldier suffered from a deficiency of Vitamin A, which rendered men night-blind—a condition noted in some letters and diaries, though the writers had no explanation for the cause. Poor Confederate night vision had already helped the Federals at Brown's Ferry and Wauhatchie; it would equally be a factor in actions yet to come.

On November 21, after receiving two telegrams from James Longstreet, Bragg reached another curious decision. Longstreet reported that he had driven the Federals into the fortifications of Knoxville, but could do little more. "I am close in under the enemy's works," he wired, "but cannot bring him to battle, as he has the other side of the river for foraging. I think that my force is hardly strong enough to warrant my taking his works by assault." In a second dispatch, Longstreet made his plea for reinforcements explicit: "Can't you spare me another division? It will shorten the work here very much."

Another view of Lookout Mountain, this from Missionary Ridge near Rossville, looking across the modern Chattanooga Valley. (dp)

More than two weeks had transpired since the Knoxville campaign began—two weeks of an increasingly narrowing window for success. Sherman's forces were now at Chattanooga, as observed by Confederate signalers atop Lookout Mountain. Almost certainly the time to reinforce Longstreet had passed; Bragg's risk was now greater than ever. However, on the 22nd, Bragg telegraphed a surprising reply: "Nearly 11,000 re-enforcements are now moving to your assistance; but if practicable to end your work with Burnside promptly and effectively, it should be done now."

Not only was Bragg suddenly going to reinforce Longstreet, but he was going to send him two divisions under one of his best officers, Maj. Gen. Patrick R. Cleburne. Simon B. Buckner's division, currently commanded by Bushrod Johnson, would move first, followed by Cleburne the next day.

Why? Bragg was gambling that with these reinforcements Longstreet could indeed finish off Burnside quickly and then return with his whole force to Chattanooga before Grant stirred himself.

For Braxton Bragg time had just run out.

James Longstreet felt glad to be out from under Braxton Bragg's thumb, but his mission to besiege Knoxville would eventually suffer because Bragg withheld necessary support. This view, says the Library of Congress, "taken after Longstreet's withdrawal on December 3, include[s] Strawberry Plains, which was on his line of retreat." (loc)

Orchard Knob

CHAPTER SEVEN

NOVEMBER 21-23, 1863

Grant remained convinced that Bragg's most vulnerable point remained the north end of Missionary Ridge. Success here would drive a blue wedge between Bragg and Longstreet. If the Federals could seize Cleveland, Tennessee, they would sever the rail connection between the two Rebel forces, dashing Confederate hopes of coordination. Since Thomas proved reluctant to move earlier in the month, Grant turned to Sherman for the task.

Grant ordered Sherman's men to cross the Tennessee at Bridgeport, follow Hooker's line of march to Brown's Ferry, cross the river again, and move among the hills on the north bank, concealed from Rebel observation. The next challenge was another pre-dawn assault crossing in pontoons, landing near the mouth of South Chickamauga Creek, where additional bridges could be erected. Once re-established back on the south bank of the Tennessee, Sherman was to strike the north end of Missionary Ridge, which, to Union observers, appeared entirely unfortified.

Thomas's and Hooker's men were only supposed to support this movement. Grant wanted the Army of the Cumberland to threaten Bragg's center while Hooker menaced Lookout Mountain. However, the

Orchard Knob rises abruptly from the valley floor about halfway between the wartime city of Chattanooga and Missionary Ridge. Initially occupied by Confederates, today it is festooned with a large number of Union monuments. (hs)

This view from the Chattanooga National Cemetery looks east towards Missionary Ridge. Once known as Bald Knob, this position and Orchard Knob marked the forward line of the Rebel infantry. (hs)

Union commander had no intention of throwing Thomas's men into a headlong assault against the main Rebel entrenchments at the foot of Missionary Ridge—a venture that promised to be bloody even if successful. Nor did it seem likely that Hooker could storm Lookout Mountain's daunting heights. Grant's trust in victory lay entirely with William Sherman and the Army of the Tennessee.

On the night of November 13, Sherman reached Bridgeport. The next day, he boarded a steamboat to Kelly's Ferry, where he was met by one of Grant's staff, who then escorted him into Chattanooga. On November 15, Grant, Sherman, and Thomas all gathered in the Union lines at Fort Wood, from whence they could observe the encircling Rebel lines.

"General Grant, you are besieged," blurted out a surprised Sherman.

Grant's reply was matter of fact: "It is too true."

In a quiet aside, Grant confided to Sherman that he feared the men of the Army of the Cumberland "were so demoralized . . . they could not be got out of their trenches to assume the offensive." Sherman's troops must lead the way.

Those troops were still toiling toward the front. After a brief rest at Bridgeport, Sherman's column resumed its march. The weather again refused to cooperate. On November 20, Pvt. Arch Brinkerhoff, and his comrades in the 4th Iowa Infantry crossed "the Tennessee River [at Bridgeport] on a pontoon bridge." They camped a mile and a half from the bridge, in the rain. The next day it was still raining. Brinkerhoff noted that "the roads" soon became "very bad." They made only seven miles.

On the 22nd, they did slightly better, "eight miles," but now the roads were "awful bad." At midnight on the 23rd, they resumed despite "roads very muddy"; by dawn, they were finally under the brow of Lookout. Near Wauhatchie, they halted again. Re-crossing the Tennessee at Brown's Ferry was proving to be slow going, so they were forced to wait for other troops to clear the way.

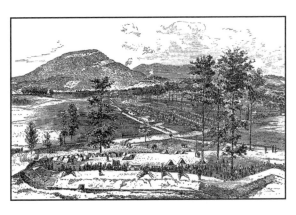

One part of those troops came from the men of the XI Corps. In keeping with his overall plan, on November 22, Grant had ordered Howard to move the corps over the Tennessee at Brown's Ferry and into Chattanooga. Grant intended to use the corps to reinforce either Thomas or Sherman, as needed, in the coming attack; as a side benefit, their easily observed movement might further confuse Bragg as to where the next blow would land. Howard reported that intercepted Confederate signals suggested the ruse worked.

After falling back from Rossville in the wake of Chickamauga, the Union army soon converted the defenses of Chattanooga into a veritable fortress. They created multiple fortified bastions, each connected by entrenchments and named for their commanders—such as Fort Grose, shown here. (b&l)

To further confuse Bragg, Grant and Sherman conspired at another piece of misdirection; Sherman's leading division first marched south toward Trenton, feigning a movement to ascend Lookout below the existing Confederate defenses. It was only a ruse, and a feeble one, given how much Confederate observers could see (on clear days, anyway) from the crest of Lookout Mountain. The unexpectedly slow progress of Sherman's column further rendered that feint ineffective.

The rain had done more than just turn the roads to quagmires. Both Brinkerhoff and Capt. Henry Kircher of the 12th Missouri served in Brig. Gen. Peter J. Osterhaus's division, bringing up Sherman's rear. Swollen with the rain, the river was running high and fast—the perfect vehicle for improvised Confederate projectiles launched into the river upstream from Brown's Ferry aimed at knocking the pontoons to pieces. Those log rafts, along with the general debris swept along by the current, repeatedly damaged the Federal bridge. Despite the best efforts of the pioneers, for much of November 23, the bridge was unusable,

An 1864 view of Bald Knob, as work was begun on the National Cemetery. George Thomas issued the orders for creation of the cemetery. When asked if the dead should be buried in sections according to their state, Thomas reputedly replied, "Mix 'em up. I am tired of States' Rights." (loc)

Union Gen. Gordon Granger commanded the IV Corps, having won fame at Chickamauga for marching to the sound of the guns and arriving in the nick of time on Snodgrass Hill. Abrasive and impolitic, Granger would not get along well with Grant. (loc)

leaving Osterhaus's men stranded on the south bank.

The delays ate at Grant. Originally, he assumed that Sherman's entire command would be ready to begin the offensive on the morning of November 21. When that date proved impossible, Grant grudgingly postponed things, instructing Sherman that "every effort must be made to get up in time to attack on Sunday morning [the 22nd.]" Now it looked like Sherman wouldn't be ready to begin his amphibious assault until the morning of the 24th, and then only by leaving Osterhaus's division far to the rear.

Grant could wait no longer. He ordered Osterhaus to join Hooker's command, strengthening the threat to Lookout Mountain; Sherman would be given use of Brig. Gen. Jefferson C. Davis's division of the XIV Corps instead.

Overnight on November 22, two Confederate deserters brought alarming news. Bragg's army was retreating, leaving, George Thomas noted, "only a strong picket line in our front." Grant's response was immediate: "to ascertain by a demonstration the truth or falsity of the report."

Fort Wood was a strong point in the center of the Union line, built upon the foundation of an earlier Confederate work. Fort Wood was named for and defended by the division of Brig. Gen. Thomas J. Wood. Several hundred yards due east of Fort Wood, halfway between Chattanooga and Missionary Ridge, rose Orchard Knob, anchoring the Confederate forward line. Thomas made that the objective of his "demonstration."

George H. Thomas believed in careful preparation, and this action would be no different. Two divisions, those of Wood and Brig. Gen. Philip H. Sheridan of Maj. Gen. Gordon Granger's IV corps, led the way. Two more divisions, drawn from Maj. Gen. John M. Palmer's XIV Corps, supported Wood:

Brig. Gen. Absalom Baird's division "refused and *en echelon*" and Brig. Gen. Richard W. Johnson's division "held in readiness . . . to re-enforce at any point." As further insurance, the 6,000 men of Howard's XI Corps were "formed *en masse*" behind Granger. The whole force advanced about 2:00 p.m.

Opposing this onslaught of approximately 14,000 Federals were a mere 634 Confederates from Brig. Gen. Arthur M. Manigault's brigade, the 24th and 28th Alabama Infantry. They were part of that "strong picket line" who had turned Orchard Knob (known as "The Cedar Hill" to the Confederates) into a forward strongpoint, "entrenched with a shallow ditch and a low earthwork."

The results were predictable, though the Rebels mounted a firmer resistance than either side expected, primarily, thought Manigault, because Maj. J. L. Butler, commander of the 28th Alabama, mistakenly believed his orders were to hold the hill "at all hazards."

The Federals soon drove off the Rebel pickets, with a sharp fight developing on the slopes of the knob. Not until the 24th when the rest of the divisional pickets gave way did Major Butler order his men to fall back—too late for some 175 of them, who fell or were captured in the fighting. On the Federal side, Wood, who bore the brunt of the fight, reported 125 losses. His objective achieved, Wood halted and awaited further instructions.

Satisfied with the movement, Grant ordered the Federals to halt and dig in. The entire fight had probably cost each side 200-300 men. Though it proved a minor affair in the war's overall calculus, most of the men in both armies could easily watch the whole affair. War had seldom been this panoramic.

To Grant, the action accomplished two things: it determined that Bragg was not retreating, and that Thomas's men would still fight.

This movement clearly caught Braxton Bragg by surprise. Bragg had no intention of abandoning his position, but he was shifting considerable forces so as to send large reinforcements to Longstreet—movements those deserters interpreted as a general retreat. Many of those troops were already chugging north along the

Union Gen. Phil Sheridan, a divisional commander under Granger, impressed Grant so much that Sheridan would travel east with Grant in 1864. (loc)

Thomas J. Wood also commanded a division under Granger. At Chickamauga, Wood famously obeyed an order, issued by Rosecrans, that opened a hole in the Union lines just as James Longstreet's Confederates attacked that very spot. (loc)

A view of the knob from the southeast. Once neglected, the knob has received more attention in recent years. (hs)

rickety rails of the Virginia & East Tennessee line. Should Bragg recall them? No, he decided; for the moment, he would continue the movement.

The Orchard Knob fight also exposed another serious weakness in the Confederate defenses. To most visitors examining the battles for Chattanooga, the crest of Missionary Ridge seems the obvious defensive ground. Heretofore, however, the main Confederate line ran along the western foot of the Ridge. There were no earthworks or improved positions at the top.

By November 23, the Confederate army had been occupying Missionary Ridge for two months. Army headquarters was located at the Moore House, slightly less than halfway along the ridge between Rossville and Tunnel Hill. But while Missionary Ridge was certainly imposing enough when viewed from the Union lines, it was a full three miles from Chattanooga, and at least two miles from the main line of Union entrenchments—too far for effective cannon fire. Moreover, the crest was narrow and the western face so steep that it proved difficult to site cannon at the military crest (the forward area of the upper slope where artillery and troops could still shoot at

In creating the battlefield park in the 1890s, organizers preserved Orchard Knob because it had been Grant's observation post for the subsequent battle of Missionary Ridge. A number of Union regiments placed their monuments here. (loc)

movement along the entire hillside). That left few good places for ridgetop defenses.

Accordingly, the main Confederate works were established at the foot, not the top. As noted, the original Rebel outpost line occupied Orchard Knob. Perhaps complacency set in, for over the previous two months, the Rebels also made no effort to prepare secondary works at the top of the ridge. Only now, on the evening of November 23, did Bragg think to order a line of works be constructed there.

Bragg's army was also now at a nadir in combat strength. His earlier detachment of Longstreet, coupled with these most recent departures, shorted him at least 20,000 men. His army was still spread across miles of terrain, including a large force on Lookout Mountain. Given that the siege was already broken, occupying Lookout served no military purpose. Shortening the lines by falling back to Missionary Ridge was the wiser course, but no orders went out to initiate that withdrawal.

Grant's luck was holding. Bragg seemed barely to be paying attention.

Battle Above the Clouds

CHAPTER EIGHT

MORNING, NOVEMBER 24, 1863

Six months previously, Union Maj. Gen. Joseph Hooker was a power to be reckoned with: commander of the Union's largest field army, a favorite of the Radical Republicans, and brimming with boastful confidence that he could "whip Bobby Lee." Defeat at Chancellorsville laid him low. Next came loss of command when, in a spat over authority, he foolishly offered up his resignation as head of the Army of the Potomac just as battle loomed in Pennsylvania. He did not expect President Lincoln to accept—but accept Lincoln did. Major General George G. Meade became the victor of Gettysburg. Hooker was sidelined.

Dispatched westward at the head of a mere fragment of the force he once wielded, Hooker feared being further relegated to the war's backwaters—which seemed to be exactly what Grant intended. When Grant detached Howard's XI Corps from Hooker to bolster Sherman, Hooker was left commanding just two undersized divisions: Geary's of the XII and Brig. Gen. Charles Cruft's of the IV Corps. Each of those commands was further reduced by the need to garrison rear areas. Sans Howard, Hooker's strength amounted to only about 7,000 men.

Unhappy with this turn of events, Hooker asked if he could personally accompany

The tangled woods and rocky hillside presented substantial difficulties for Geary's men as they moved to attack. Ravines, boulders, and increasingly steep slopes all broke up formations and separated units. (dp)

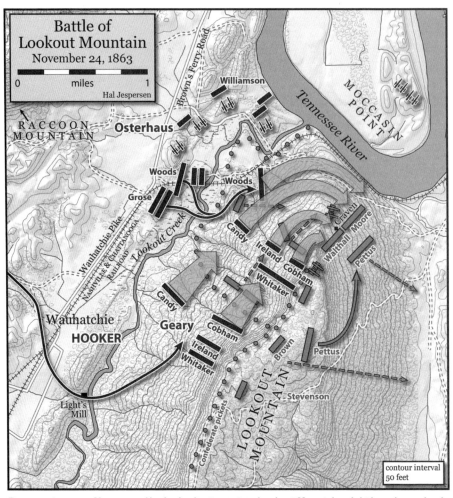

BATTLE OF LOOKOUT MOUNTAIN—Hooker's plan to capture Lookout Mountain might have been simple in concept, but it proved tricky to execute. While Osterhaus's division and Grose's brigade feinted an attack directly across Lookout Creek at the railroad bridge, Geary's division sidled south to cross the creek at Light's Mill. From there, they swept north along the face of the mountain's lower slopes, outflanking the defenders. Not only did Geary face extremely difficult terrain, he also had to depend on the mist, rain, and clouds to hide his movement from premature discovery.

Howard's corps, where he might at least get a chance to get into the fight. Instead, George Thomas instructed him to remain in Lookout Valley. There, per Grant's wishes, Hooker's only mission was to "make demonstrations [as] early as possible after daybreak [on November 24,] on [the] point of Lookout Mountain."

Then fate lent a hand. The bridge problems at Brown's Ferry left Osterhaus's men stranded on

This view shows Lookout Mountain from near where Gen. Hooker watched the action, and from where artists Theodore Davis and James Walker sketched and painted their own versions of the fight. (hs)

the wrong bank of the Tennessee. Here Grant's impatience worked in Hooker's favor. Refusing to delay Sherman's assault any longer, Grant agreed instead to attach Osterhaus's 4,000 men to Hooker's command. If Osterhaus couldn't get across the river and catch up to Sherman by November 24, then Hooker could expand his own mission: "You can take the point of Lookout if your demonstration develops its practicability." That grudging latitude proved to be all the permission Hooker needed.

Brigadier General Peter J. Osterhaus had just returned to the army after a sad furlough. On November 10, he was in St. Louis, burying his wife, Matilda. She perished unexpectedly— per one newspaper, she collapsed after reading a garbled account of her husband's death in battle—leaving Osterhaus to make arrangements for their five young children. Osterhaus and his family were German émigrés, with no relations America, so the children were placed with friends until Matilda's unmarried sister, Amalie, could come from Germany to help. Then Osterhaus rushed back to the army.

He caught up to his men on November 22 as they trudged toward Brown's Ferry. The next night he conferred with Hooker, where he learned of the new mission. Hooker, who hadn't enjoyed good relations with Germans in Federal uniform back east—he blamed the largely-German XI Corps for his discomfiture at Chancellorsville—nonetheless found Osterhaus to be "a glorious soldier . . . the best representative of the European service it has been my fortune to be become acquainted with."

For his part, Osterhaus recalled that, as it neared midnight, Hooker recounted that Grant had "abandon[ed] the scheme of a feint . . . and with the assistance of my Division [Hooker planned] to attack and dislodge the Rebels from their Lookout positions." Fighting Joe Hooker intended much more than a "demonstration."

Charged with Lookout's defense, Confederate Maj. Gen. Carter L. Stevenson faced a daunting task. Lookout Mountain was a long ridge, stretching nearly 100 miles in length. Its southern end began in Alabama, running northeast until its northern peak towered over the Tennessee River and the city of Chattanooga. At that northern terminus, Lookout stood 1,850 feet above sea level, and 1,100 feet above the city below.

The lower third of the mountain sloped ruggedly up to a narrow plateau, on which sat the luxurious home of Robert Cravens, a prosperous local businessman, surrounded by 88 acres of level shelf-land. The remaining two thirds of the mountain rose in even steeper slopes until they became vertical rock walls—the oft-described palisades. Worse still, thanks to that vertical palisade, troops could not readily move between shelf and summit. Nor could artillery on top of the mountain do much to support men fighting on the shelf or lower slopes. In effect, units above and below the palisade were isolated from each other.

Prior to November 23, the Confederates had three divisions placed to defend Lookout Mountain. Carter Stevenson's division replaced Longstreet's men in defending the crest. Major

Newly arrived from East Tennessee, Confederate divisional commander Carter Stevenson was assigned the difficult responsibility of defending Lookout Mountain. Stevenson's last combat assignment had been at Vicksburg, where he was captured in July 1863. (loc)

General W. H. T. Walker's division defended a line at the mountain's foot, from Chattanooga Creek to Lookout's western slopes as far as Lookout Creek. Cheatham's division, currently commanded by Brig. Gen. John K. Jackson, occupied the Cravens House bench. The whole force was part of Lt. Gen. William J. Hardee's Corps, with Hardee making his headquarters on a modest rise just east of Chattanooga Creek.

Then circumstances changed. Confederates clearly observed Sherman's and Howard's movements across the Tennessee at Brown's Ferry, inducing Bragg to expect an attack on his now-weakened right flank (recall that Cleburne's and Buckner's divisions were departing for East Tennessee at this time.) Accordingly, Bragg ordered Hardee to lead Walker's division over to Missionary Ridge and take personal command there.

Hardee's departure left Stevenson in overall charge, tasked with defending everything west of Chattanooga Creek: mountain, shelf, and valley. Only six brigades were now available for the task: the three comprising Stevenson's own division and three more in Jackson's command.

Stevenson detached Brig. Gen. Alfred Cumming's Georgia brigade and, combining it with Jackson's own brigade, moved both off the Cravens bench to replace Walker. This move in effect created a new ad-hoc demi-division under Cumming's command, he being the senior officer. Jackson was left to command Cheatham's now-reduced division of two brigades—Brig. Gen. Edward C. Walthall's 1,200 Mississippians and Brig. Gen. John C. Moore's 1,000 Alabamans— at the Cravens House, relying more on the extremely rugged nature of the lower slopes than in any troop strength to stymie an attacker. Walthall deployed his men on the northwestern slopes of Lookout, facing Hooker, while those of Moore's men not dispatched to the picket line remained just east of the house in reserve.

Stevenson placed his last two brigades atop the mountain, oriented mainly to defend against a

Edward Cary Walthall was a Mississippi lawyer with a proven talent for combat. He led his brigade into ferocious fighting at Chickamauga, performing well. By the end of the war he would rise to divisional command, and (very briefly) a much-attenuated corps command. (loc)

Union approach from the south, along the broad plateau of Lookout's crest. Despite Hardee's advice to the contrary, Stevenson elected to keep his headquarters atop the mountain, for Lookout's towering height provided the best view. However, with Stevenson at the crest and Jackson dividing his time between the valley and the bench, no single commander exercised firm control of the Cravens House sector.

Stevenson knew he was stretched far too thinly to securely hold all points. On November 23, he relayed his concerns to Bragg via signal flag, fearing an attack on his forces the next day. That message, visible to Union signalers as well as Bragg's people on Missionary Ridge, was soon decoded. Grant and Thomas decided to exacerbate those worries. At 10 p.m. that evening, based in part on that intercept, Thomas informed Hooker that "the general commanding department [Grant] directs that you endeavor to take the point of Lookout Mountain."

The "demonstration" was now a full-fledged attack.

Finding Lookout Creek too deep to wade, Geary's men improvised a footbridge here near Light's Mill. It took several hours to get the division across the creek and deployed for action. (dp)

* * *

November 24 dawned damp and foggy. Hooker advanced his artillery and one brigade of Cruft's division toward the face of the Cravens House shelf from the northwest, but he had no intention of attacking head on. Geary's division, reinforced with Cruft's other brigade, would deliver the main blow. Geary's column moved south through Lookout Valley to the vicinity of Light's Mill.

After capturing a Rebel picket post, Geary's men crossed Lookout Creek on a hastily constructed bridge, one regiment at a time. As they crossed, a member of the 149th New York noted that "gen. Geary, standing on the bank,

Michael Light purchased the mill from Casper Vaughn in the 1830s, during the Cherokee Removal. The Light family continued to operate the mill at the time of the war. According to the sign erected at Reflection Riding Nature Center, these are the original millstones, though little other information about the Light family has been uncovered. See page 128 for GPS coordinates. (hs)

shook hands with the colonel of each regiment, and gave him his orders."

Once across, the column ascended the lower slope of Lookout as far as the palisade wall. Then soldiers deployed facing north, taking up a line outflanking Walthall's defenders. In the meantime, Osterhaus's men advanced to support and strengthen Cruft's feint. To aid in that deception, Union pioneers began trying to bridge Lookout Creek in two other locations. Once Geary's men attacked, both Cruft's remaining force and Osterhaus's men were to cross the watercourse and join in.

The dense, patchy fog and low clouds greatly aided the Federals. Stevenson visited Walthall at first light. In his view, the lower slopes were indefensible because any Confederate lines on the north or northwest faces of the mountain were dominated by a Union artillery sited both on the hills just west of Lookout Creek and from Moccasin Bend. If attacked, Walthall was to fall back on Moore.

Walthall's five regiments were widely dispersed, supporting his extended picket line.

This rock wall was erected by some of Longstreet's men when they were tasked with defending Lookout Mountain, then later inherited by the Mississippians. Note that it faced west, looking down the mountain, but Geary's men struck the wall perpendicularly, facing the camera, outflanking the defenders. (dp)

The 29th and 30th Mississippi were farthest along the western face of the mountain, occupying a rock wall, facing west, in works previously constructed by Longstreet's men. Collectively, their orders were to support the pickets running from the palisade down the lower slope to the creek. The 24th, 27th, and that part of the 34th Mississippi not already on the picket line were stationed nearer the Cravens House plateau. A lawyer by profession, Walthall was an effective citizen-soldier who had most recently fought extremely well at Chickamauga; the challenges would be greater here.

After Stevenson left for the mountain's crest, Walthall and Moore tried to puzzle out the barely glimpsed and fragmentary Union movements observed below. The fog grew denser through the morning, limiting their view, but sometime between 8 and 9 a.m., they saw either Col. Charles R. Woods's brigade (of Osterhaus) or Col. William Grose's brigade (of Cruft) deploying near the destroyed railroad bridge over Lookout Creek.

Walthall ordered the remainder of the 34th forward to reinforce his pickets near the rail and road bridge sites over Lookout Creek, where Federals threatened a crossing. In the meantime,

Moore carried word of this enemy activity back to General Jackson and then returned to his own headquarters at the intersection of the Summertown and Cravens House roads. Jackson in turn relayed the news to Stevenson, but his own personal observations seemed to contradict those of his two brigadiers. He "walked out" to "a favorable point" where he could observe the main Federal position in front of Chattanooga, only to discover "all quiet, no massing, no movements of any kind." Of course, he was looking in the wrong place—east of the mountain, not west.

Hooker's plan progressed slowly, but effectively. It took Geary several hours to cross the creek and ascend the lower slopes. He deployed his own division in the first line. Colonel George A. Cobham's small two-regiment Pennsylvania brigade held the right, highest on the slope and adjacent to the palisade. Three of Col. David Ireland's New York regiments came next, with a fourth, the 102nd New York, deployed as skirmishers. Colonel Charles Candy's five regiments, a mix of Ohio and Pennsylvania men, anchored the left. Behind these roughly 3,000 easterners, Geary formed Brig. Gen. Walter C. Whitaker's large brigade in two lines, six regiments comprising another 2,000 bayonets. At around 11:00 a.m., Geary led the entire mass forward.

They first struck Walthall's pickets, who promptly fell back toward the 29th and 30th Mississippi. The rock wall defense immediately proved useless: it was facing the wrong way. "To our joy," later wrote Sgt. Charles Partridge of the 96th Illinois, "we saw that [their works] had been constructed to resist a direct attack from below, and that from our position we could rake them with an enfilading fire."

Major James M. Johnson, commanding the 30th Mississippi, was the first to be assailed. In truth, virtually all of Johnson's men, "under orders from" Walthall, were already deployed so thinly they amounted to no more than a second skirmish line; their fire, delivered at a range of

Peter J. Osterhaus was another German-American in blue, although not with the XI Corps. A Rhenish Prussian by birth, he embraced the liberal tide that swept across Europe in 1848, then fled to America when that revolt failed. Osterhaus proved an extremely capable field commander. (loc)

This view, looking east with the Grose marker in the foreground, shows the flat creek bottomland where Grose's men first encountered Rebel skirmishers. The lower slopes of Lookout rise at the far edge of the field. (hs)

150 yards, only "checked [the Federals] for two or three moments." Once Colonel Cobham's Pennsylvanians—who had pushed ahead of the rest of Geary's line—realized Johnson's weakness, they "drove the regiment back precipitously on the Twenty-ninth Mississippi."

Those Mississippians fared no better. Colonel William F. Brantly, commanding the 29th, ordered the regiment to change front to the southwest, but again, his numbers were lacking. Colonel William Rickards of the 29th Pennsylvania commanding Geary's right flank, hard against the palisade, saw an opportunity. Ordering a charge, "the first line advanced at the double-quick, dislodging the enemy from his position, killing and wounding several and capturing many."

Brantly mournfully concurred: "the enemy was upon me in four lines, and soon succeeded in driving me from my position, and in capturing a great many of my men." Those Mississippians fortunate enough to get away unscathed fell back on the line of the 24th and 27th Mississippi, some distance to the rear.

These two regiments, with more time to re-deploy, mounted stiffer resistance. For a moment, the Rebels seemed to prevail. Lieutenant Colonel A. J. Jones of the 27th Mississippi reported that his men "poured into their advancing columns a terrible fire," so destructive that "soon their lines . . . broke and retreated. . . . I saw one stand of the enemy's colors twice fall." The check proved momentary. Once again, the Rebels were discomfited by their lack of numbers. Captain George Collins of the 149th New York, facing this fire, recalled that "the right of [our] line extended so far up the mountain that it overlapped the [enemy's] rifle pits, and before the enemy was aware of it, he was flanked."

Understanding that he was already woefully outnumbered before the 24th Mississippi was engaged, Walthall anticipated the need for another fallback position. He ordered Col. William F. Dowd of the 24th to detach three—and shortly thereafter a fourth—companies of "sharpshooters" and place them in line about 300 yards to the rear. Coupled with Dowd's earlier orders to send additional men forward to reinforce the picket line, this move left Dowd with only two companies with which to support the 27th. Their line was soon overlapped on both flanks.

Atop the mountain, Carter Stevenson attempted to support Walthall with a line of sharpshooters, and even some cannon, lining the crest to try to fire down into Geary's formations. That fire never amounted to more than a nuisance, however, and was wholly ineffective against the 29th and 111th Pennsylvania, uppermost on the slope and doing the flanking. Directed by their brigade commander, Colonel Cobham, the Keystoners worked their way forward along the base of the palisade, turning the Mississippians' left, which gave the rest of Geary's line a chance to regroup. "As a result the enemy broke and ran," wrote Captain Collins, observing from lower down, "and captures were made by the hundred."

Two divisions of Union soldiers including regiments from Illinois, Indiana, Iowa, Kentucky, Missouri, and Ohio passed here on November 24, 1863, on their way to reinforce others already engaged with Confederates on Lookout Mountain. This marker in Reflection Riding Arboretum and Nature Center denotes the passage of Grose's Brigade. (hs)

Now Walthall's men were everywhere fleeing, scrambling down the slope toward the Tennessee River or back toward the Cravens farmstead, where Walthall hoped to make a third stand long enough for reinforcements to reach him. The Federals pursued equally wildly.

Not only did Geary's line rally and give chase, but now both brigades of Osterhaus's division entered the fray. As the Rebel pickets along the creek retreated, Osterhaus's men followed. Woods's brigade moved against Walthall's right, outflanking the 34th Mississippi at the bridge sites. So busy were the Mississippians with two of Grose's regiments, the 75th and 84th Illinois, that Woods's appearance caught them by surprise, resulting in the capture of nearly the entire regiment. Osterhaus personally led James A. Williamson's large Iowa brigade up "the mountain in as direct a line as possible, in order to reach the right of . . . Wood's brigade and press the enemy toward him." Osterhaus's movement leveraged hundreds of Rebels from Walthall and Moore's extended picket line away from the rest of the brigade, adding 225 of Moore's Alabamians to the day's captures.

Walthall ordered a general retreat to Cravens House, an instruction that was already outpaced by events. His men fell back across the exposed northern shoulder of the mountain just as the fog was lifting, allowing the Union artillery positioned on the hills west of Lookout Creek and on Moccasin Bend to open fire, further exacerbating Walthall's problems. That fire, said Walthall, "produced confusion" as his men retired, especially from the bend, where the Federal cannon delivered a wicked crossfire along the length of the Mississippians' retreat route and played hell with Dowd's four companies of the 24th in their fallback position. Instead of rallying for another stand, most of those men fortunate enough to escape kept going across the plateau.

In their retreat, they rushed past and through two Confederate cannon stationed in Mr. Cravens's yard. Those guns were one section of Capt. Evan P. Howell's Georgia Battery, commanded by Lt. R. T. Gibson, who now found himself in a bad fix. With his field of fire masked by fleeing Confederates, Gibson was unable to engage the enemy. Nor could he limber and depart; his battery horses were currently down in the valley, getting water. With no way to save his guns, Gibson ordered his crews away, letting the pieces fall into jubilant Federal hands.

The Fight for Cravens House

CHAPTER NINE

AFTERNOON AND EVENING,
NOVEMBER 24, 1863

This modern image demonstrates how little effect Confederate troops atop Lookout's summit could have on the fighting raging below. Even on a clear day, the distance is too great, and the slope too steep, to deliver effective fire. With fog and mist swirling around the mountain, there was little hope of checking the Union attack from above. (dp)

Neither Confederate Gen. Carter Stevenson nor John K. Jackson contributed much to the battle of Lookout Mountain on November 24. Initially, the fog masked the extent of the Union threat, but both Stevenson and Jackson also fundamentally discounted the idea of an attack from the west. Stevenson regarded Walthall's forward position as indefensible anyway, thanks to the Union artillery, and never intended for Walthall to do much more than fight a delaying action. He worried more about a thrust from the south, against the crest.

General Jackson remained equally passive. When he could see no Union threat emerging against the east side of the mountain, he waited to see what would happen next. Jackson believed that any attack would come with plenty of warning: "I expected, from the rugged nature of the ground, and the fact that the enemy had to ascend the mountain, that the picket fighting would continue for some time before the main body would be engaged." He was wrong.

When and if Walthall was attacked, as per Stevenson's intent, Jackson expected the

A peaceful scene today, on November 24 the Cravens farmstead and orchard were the scene of intense fighting. The house was destroyed, to be rebuilt after the war. (dp)

Confederate Gen. John K. Jackson, a lawyer from Augusta, Georgia, before the war, led a brigade at Shiloh, Stones River, and Chickamauga. He was a competent if not spectacular brigade commander. He did not shine at Lookout Mountain. (ph)

Mississippians to conduct a retrograde skirmishing action back to the Cravens bench. There, thought Jackson, Walthall would form the divisional right, upslope from Cravens House, with Col. John C. Moore's Alabama brigade falling in on the left, "prolonging the line in the works below the Cravens house as far as his troops would extend."

Well enough, but Jackson did little to anticipate that need. At mid-morning, when Stevenson sent Jackson a courier asking if reinforcements were needed—Stevenson had most of a brigade under Brig. Gen. Edmund W. Pettus available to send—Jackson declined since no obvious threat had yet materialized. Some time later, when Moore sent word that he did not know where to form, Jackson replied as quoted above but made no move to either personally show Moore where to go or order Moore into a specific position.

Then at noon, everything seemed to happen at once. First came word from Moore, via his pickets, that Union troops were threatening to cross Lookout Creek near the railroad bridge. Almost immediately thereafter, word arrived that Walthall was attacked. Then came a courier from Stevenson, informing Jackson of the same assault, based largely on the sounds wafting up the mountain from below. Jackson returned Stevenson's courier post-haste, asking for those reinforcements, and ordered Moore into action. Those tasks completed, Jackson rode toward the Cravens House to see what was happening for himself.

On the way, he first passed Moore's men and then met a flood of stragglers: Walthall's routed Mississippians. These were followed by a courier from Walthall, reporting the now-evident fact that Walthall's "brigade had been driven back in considerable confusion." At this juncture, another of Jackson's staff officers arrived with a request from Moore, who wished "to have a full supply of ammunition" before going into action—a surprising detail indeed given that Moore's men were supposed to have been standing ready since 9:00 a.m. that morning.

This and other overlooked details suggest that Jackson and Moore were both negligent that morning. Jackson should have met with both Walthall and Moore to survey the intended battleground, allowing Moore to see where his position would be and how he would co-ordinate with Walthall's people. Even if Jackson didn't oversee such a survey, why didn't Moore at least ride up as far as Cravens House to view the trench line Jackson intended him to defend? As importantly, why, at noon, were Moore's men still lacking sufficient ammunition? They had only 30 rounds apiece, when they should have entered combat with at least 100 rounds per man.

Nonetheless, Moore pressed on, meeting that same jumble of Walthall's men on the way. "To my utter astonishment," Moore reported, still short "300 or 400 yards" from the intended works, "the enemy . . . had . . . occupied a portion of the trenches of my brigade."

"We moved forward to occupy the line," recalled Sgt. Samuel Sprott of the 40th Alabama, "[but] . . . we found the enemy in possession of a part of it, whereupon that part of our line fell back . . ." A second Rebel "rush for the works," however, sent the Federals back in turn.

By now, Geary's troops were quickly wearing down, badly disorganized and exhausted by the long running fight over such difficult terrain. Cobham's and some of Ireland's men met and overwhelmed Colonel Dowd's last four companies of the 24th

John C. Moore was a West Pointer who resigned his commission in 1855. At the start of the war, he was sent first to Texas, then joined Albert Sidney Johnston's army in time to fight at Shiloh. He was captured at Vicksburg. He would resign his Confederate commission in early 1864 after butting heads with Gen. Hardee. (ph)

Theodore Davis's illustration of the battle of Lookout Mountain bears many similarities to James Walker's later paintings of the same subject. There is a Union battery engaged to the image's right, a gathering of staff officers to the left, and even a man on a rearing white horse in the left-center, which might be Joe Hooker. (hw)

Mississippi, posted just west of the Cravens's farmyard. It was another short, sharp engagement. Dowd reached this line shortly after the combined 27th/24th line crumbled, and though Walthall had ordered him "to hold my post till Hell froze over," to Dowd it now looked like "the ice was about five feet over it." Once again, Moccasin Bend's Federal artillery raked this last line, and once again Colonel Rickard's 29th Pennsylvania turned Dowd's flank near the palisade. Another 150 Rebels surrendered.

Parts of two more of Ireland's regiments, the 60th and 137th New York, swept on to claim the capture of Lt. R. T. Griffiths's two Confederate cannon, the first of a set of conflicting trophy claims that would be disputed for decades at reunions and in veterans' newspapers. The rest of Ireland's men—indeed, Geary's whole division—were now scattered back across the line of attack. Colonel Candy's brigade, lowest on the slope and initially diverted to clear the east bank of Lookout Creek in order to facilitate Grose's and Osterhaus's crossings, lagged the farthest.

Another wartime illustration, this image shows a line of works in Union hands, with fighting around Cravens House still raging in the background. (hw)

Thus, when Moore's men appeared, they caught the Federals at a disadvantage. The fog and rain had again thickened. Lieutenant Colonel Charles B. Randall, commanding the 149th New York, thought "it was impossible to distinguish clearly the movements of the enemy or of our own troops. . . ." Fearing a move against their left, the 149th, and then the rest of Ireland's command, began to retreat. Equally uncertain of the circumstances, Moore halted his line partly behind a stone wall and partly in the trenches, only to discover, as Sergeant Sprott related, that these "were practically worthless, as the entire line was exposed to a raking fire on Moccasin Point." Even worse, Federals still occupied the upward portion of the line, which was originally supposed to have been held by Walthall. As a result, reported Moore, "they completely enfiladed my left."

Here the fight might have lapsed into a lull, each side lacking the momentum to press farther, if not for Brig. Gen. Walter C. Whitaker's command. Whitaker's six Union regiments had so far not been

Gen. Whitaker, another lawyer, commanded the 6th Kentucky Infantry before rising to brigade command. Despite postwar accusations of drunkenness, Whitaker was never censured at the time and would continue to command his brigade until 1864. He was wounded at Resaca and promoted to divisional command thereafter. (ph)

engaged, though they had been subject to fire from Stevenson's men atop the mountain and whatever overshooting Walthall's troops delivered. Formed in two lines, Whitaker followed Geary's men across the west face of the mountain.

The first of Whitaker's regiments to reach the scene at Cravens House was the 40th Ohio. Without orders, Col. Jacob E. Taylor led his Buckeyes through and past Ireland's men, racing toward the white clapboard walls of Cravens House to seize the two abandoned Confederate cannon standing in the yard. The Alabamians comprising Moore's left, witnessing this move, opened an accurate fire. The 40th lost thirty men here, twelve of them killed, most at the outset of the advance. Then the Ohioans stalled around the house and cannon, returning fire. Their position was precarious. For a moment it looked like Moore's men might flank them on their left.

At this point, Whitaker tried to arrest any further advance. He attempted to stop two more of his regiments, the 99th Ohio and the 35th "First Irish" Indiana, at the line of Ireland's re-organizing brigade, to no avail. As each regiment surged past him, Whitaker reversed course and urged them forward. Captain Harrison Shuey of the 99th thought it a sound move: "our sagacious commander . . . ordered us to charge forward and prevent them from forming. With a shout our brigade rushed forward, passing through the first line" to front against Moore's breastworks on the 99th's left.

Similarly, Col. Bernard F. Mullen of the Indiana Irish, "believing it important to push on with the right of our line," came pounding up in the 99th's right. Some of those Hoosiers overran Griffith's two cannon, claiming the captures for themselves. However, after the battle Mullen graciously turned those guns over to the 40th Ohio, allowing the Buckeyes to strengthen their own assertion of credit.

With half his brigade already engaged, Whitaker fully abandoned all thought of stopping.

He ordered Col. Thomas Champion of the 96th Illinois, currently commanding the reserve line of his own regiment and the 51st Ohio, to clear the upper plateau and turn Moore's left. Champion's line scrambled to comply and soon delivered a wicked fire against Moore's naked left flank.

Moore thought it high time to depart. Sergeant Sprott thought that he and his fellow Alabamians were doing fine work, having "repuls[ed] the enemy handsomely several times," when Moore ordered a retreat. The Confederates fell back in a southeasterly direction, clockwise around the east side of the mountain, until they came to Walthall and a fragment of his command rallied into a new line. Moore fell in alongside. Jackson's intended two-brigade line (such as it was) formed at last.

Though the shooting would continue until past nightfall, by 2:00 p.m., the battle was essentially over. While some Federals wanted to renew the attack, Hooker had no intention of pressing his luck. So far, all the fighting had been within view—albeit intermittently, thanks to the rain and mists—of the powerful array of Union supporting artillery. Once they passed beyond the point of Lookout and onto its eastern face, however, that support was blocked by the mountain's bulk. When Whitaker met Col. William Grose toiling up the mountain with his brigade, he ordered Grose to renew the attack. Grose declined, showing Whitaker a written order from Hooker instructing him to halt near Cravens House. Both sides reinforced their existing lines, but neither side

This view shows Cravens House as Gen. Moore would have seen it, from below. Moore expected to fall in on Walthall's right, but the Mississippians did not reform as Moore expected. (dp)

This image shows Cravens House from above, where Colonel Champion of the 96th Illinois turned Moore's left, and where later, some of Col. Cobham's men joined in that movement. (dp)

Here Moore's and Walthall's men finally rallied, just preventing the Federals from seizing Summertown Road. Had they done so, the remaining Rebels atop Lookout would have been effectively isolated from the army. (dp)

made any real effort to drive the other. The one significant consequence of Hooker's decision was that the Summertown Road—the only rapid way down off the mountain for Stevenson's remaining men—remained in Confederate hands.

The firing, however, didn't abate. Over the course of the afternoon, each side believed it had checked several determined attacks. "Here we repulsed every effort made by the enemy to dislodge us," boasted Samuel Sprott. Brigadier General Edmund Pettus, who finally arrived and replaced Walthall's battered remnant on Moore's left, concurred: "The enemy made repeated assaults on my left, but were bravely met and repulsed by the Twentieth Alabama Regiment and four companies of the Thirty-first . . . ."

The intensity of the firing was partially explained by one of Colonel Ireland's aides, Lt. Albert Greene, as an overreaction to Union reinforcements. At one point Colonel Candy's brigade arrived and took position on the line, replacing Ireland's New Yorkers, who had come up in Whitaker's wake. "The movement of getting them in and our men out," wrote Greene, "attracted the attention of the enemy, and they opened a heavy fire. The lead came fearfully for ten or fifteen minutes. . . . This firing has been spoken of as a charge by the rebels, but they did not come out of their works, firing rather to repel what they imagined was going to be an assault."

At 8:00 p.m., with full dark, the Rebels withdrew. With Cravens House plateau now in Union hands and the Summertown Road endangered, Stevenson's remaining force atop the mountain was imperiled. Bragg decided that he could no longer risk losing the force required to hold Lookout Mountain. The remaining troops atop the mountain, posted at the Cravens House plateau and strung across Lookout Creek, all fell back to Missionary Ridge, where Bragg determined to make his next stand.

Results

CHAPTER TEN

The battle for Lookout Mountain did not decide the fate of Chattanooga. It was instead the dramatic first act of Grant's larger plan to defeat or destroy Bragg's Army of Tennessee—and even then, a last-minute addition to the playbook. Had Peter Osterhaus's division crossed the Tennessee River with the rest of Sherman's column, the battle likely never would have been fought.

But fought it was, and most memorably, too. Hooker's plan worked masterfully, aided by the fog and mist that shrouded much of his activity and left the Confederates confused and uncertain about where a Federal blow might land. That same fog parted dramatically, at what seemed to be just the right moment, to reveal glimpses of the day's events to the assembled multitudes watching in both armies.

The battle also spawned a subsequent war of words. Four separate Union regiments laid claim to capturing the two Confederate cannon abandoned at Cravens House. Members of the 60th and 137th New York certainly bickered among themselves about who deserved the credit, but they united in opposing the 40th Ohio's and 35th Indiana's similar boasts, not the least because the latter two regiments were not Army of the Potomac expatriates.

That rivalry extended between generals, as well. In their reports, Colonel Ireland and General Geary never acknowledged that Whitaker's brigade

This monument to the 147th Pennsylvania is placed on a ledge above Cravens House, where it sits with several other markers, including the 96th Illinois's stone. Col. Ario Pardee has another distinction to his name: Pardee Field on the lower slope of Culp's Hill, at Gettysburg, is named for him. (hs)

This Iowa Memorial is only one of several large monuments erected to commemorate the battle of Lookout Mountain. Ohio erected a similar shaft nearby. New York put up two: one at Cravens House and one at the summit. There are also a number of regimental markers and war department tablets. (dp)

Col. David Ireland of the 137th New York ably led his brigade into action on November 24. Ireland is probably best known for his highly capable defense of Culp's Hill at Gettysburg earlier that year on July 2. Ireland would not survive the war. Though he was wounded several times, it was dysentery that took his life on September 10, 1864. (bb)

played a role. In 1890, Albert Greene depicted the entire battle as having been won by Ireland's men, charging on heedless of circumstances. After finally butting up against the Confederate final line, said Greene, "Ireland told me to go back and look for help. . . . I went back to the white house, and there found one Brigadier General Whitaker, who with a brigade had gotten onto the plateau somehow. Whitaker was drunk; not fighting drunk, but complacently so. . . . I tried to explain our urgent needs . . . [but] he replied that his troops had carried the mountain, and had gone into camp, and that the battle was over." Nonplussed, Greene claimed he returned and explained this to "Ireland, who went to Whitaker begging aid. But all the aid that Whitaker would render was to offer a drink out of an enormous flask that he had slung on him. The two had a very sharp quarrel; but the tipsy brigadier persisted that the battle was over . . . ."

To be sure, Whitaker had a reputation as a drinker. Charles A. Dana accused him of being "drunk and disorderly" at Brown's Ferry on November 1. But there also can be no denying that Whitaker's men were hotly engaged around Cravens House, or that Whitaker was sufficiently alert to deploy his reserve line at the right moment, or even that it was Whitaker who urged Colonel Grose to renew the attack. Greene's post-war memory of what happened was nearly as shrouded by fog as was the battlefield on the day of the fight.

The battle cost the Federals 671 casualties, the Confederates 1,251—of which roughly 1,000 were captured.

In later years, Joe Hooker would make much of the engagement and his role in it, including commissioning a massive canvas depicting the fight, with himself at the center of the action. At least in part as a response to Hooker's braggadocio, Grant downplayed the affair, dismissing it in his memoirs as "one of the romances of the war."

However, the fight clearly had a dramatic impact on the tens of thousands of men watching. While clouds, fog, and rain obscured most of the action, periodically that blanket would lift, revealing fleeting glimpses of a panoramic combat to the mesmerized audience. That weather also gave the battle its sobriquet. In a telegram to Washington that evening, Union Brig. Gen. Montgomery Meigs reported that "the day had been one of driving mists and rains, and much of Hooker's battle was fought above the clouds, which concealed him from our view, but from which his musketry was heard."

Assistant Secretary of War Charles A. Dana was present through the fighting for Chattanooga. He is pictured here with Grant's army in Virginia in 1864. (loc)

But Bragg was not gone. Instead his army clung stubbornly to Missionary Ridge although any hope of successfully besieging the Federals in Chattanooga was now laid to rest. Why did Bragg remain? Probably for reasons never fully articulated: Because the victory at Chickamauga would seem for naught if he retreated; because Bragg had been harshly criticized for abrupt retreats in the past, in Kentucky, at Murfreesboro, and at Tullahoma; and because there was a good chance that an unsatisfactory result at Chattanooga would see Braxton Bragg relieved from command. Failure was in the wind, and Bragg was perhaps determined this time to stand and fight.

And a fight he would have. November 24, 1863, was a dramatic day; November 25 promised equal drama. The Union now arrayed nearly 80,000 troops at Chattanooga, and so far, less than a quarter of those had yet seen action.

Ulysses S. Grant intended a much larger battle the next day.

Despite the fact that Grant later downplayed the struggle for Lookout Mountain, he was no more immune to the mountain's lure than any other soldier. This image is one of the more iconic photographs to come out of the Civil War: Grant seeing the sights atop Lookout Mountain. (loc)

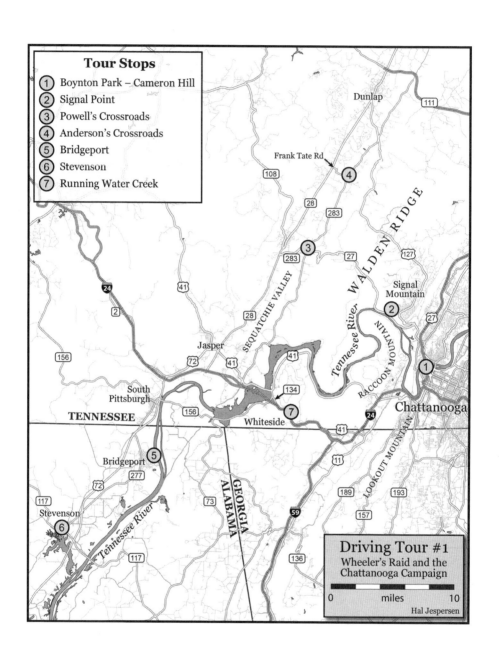

Tour Stops

1. Boynton Park – Cameron Hill
2. Signal Point
3. Powell's Crossroads
4. Anderson's Crossroads
5. Bridgeport
6. Stevenson
7. Running Water Creek

Driving Tour #1
Wheeler's Raid and the
Chattanooga Campaign

0   miles   10

Hal Jespersen

Wheeler's Raid and the Chattanooga Campaign

DRIVING TOUR 1

This tour requires a great deal of driving and will take most of a day to complete. It is meant to take you to some of the more out-of-the-way places associated with the Chattanooga Campaign and involves travel across Georgia, Tennessee, and Alabama.

The tour begins at the Chickamauga-Chattanooga National Military Park (CCNMP) headquarters, Fort Oglethorpe, Georgia.

GPS: N 34.94043, W 85.25994

▶ To Tour Stop 1

Exit the park headquarters and turn left onto LaFayette Rd. North of the park this road becomes US Rte 27 North. Stay on US 27 N until it merges with US Interstate 24 West (I-24.) Follow I-24/US 27 until 27 exits right at exit 1A, and take that to the Martin Luther King Blvd. exit. At the bottom of the ramp, turn left onto Martin Luther King Blvd.

Travel approximately 0.5 miles to Gateway Ave., and turn right. Travel another 0.25 miles and turn left onto Cameron Hill Circle. You will see the main entrance and security gate for Blue Cross Blue Shield Tennessee ahead and, just to the right, the small parking area for Boynton Park.

GPS: N 35.05398, W 85.31647

At Boynton Park—Cameron Hill

Cameron Hill, once much higher, was the site of both Confederate and Union fortifications. Today this small public park is all that remains. (hs)

You are standing on what is left of Cameron Hill, facing north, overlooking the city of Chattanooga. In 1863, Cameron Hill was much higher and contained an earthwork fort. Both the Confederates and then the Federals occupied the fort and placed artillery here. Cameron Hill was greatly reduced in the 1960s when much of it was used as fill to create the right-of-way for the new highway, I-24, along the foot of Lookout Mountain, which is to your left-rear. Across the river is Stringer's Ridge, from where Union artillery first shelled Rebel-occupied Chattanooga in August 1863. The 1863 town of Chattanooga numbered 2,500 people in 1860, and extended from the river to about 9th Street, close to where you exited 27 onto MLK Blvd.

→ **To Tour Stop 2**

Head back south on Cameron Hill Circle Dr., and turn right at Gateway Dr. Turn left onto MLK Blvd., and then bear right onto the US 27 N entrance ramp. Follow US 27 N to the Signal Mountain Rd. exit, exit right, and then turn left onto Signal Mountain Rd. Follow Signal Mountain Rd (also known as US 127) up the mountain to Signal Mountain Blvd., and turn left.

At the next intersection, turn left onto Mississippi Ave. In 0.8 miles, Mississippi Ave. will intersect with James Blvd., proceed straight ahead onto James Blvd. In

0.2 miles, you will intersect with Signal Mountain Blvd. again (to the right) and Signal Point Rd. (to the left). Turn left onto Signal Point Rd. The road will end at Signal Point Park.

GPS: N 35.12066, W 85.36641

Signal Point, often overlooked, is the most remote of the units run by the Chickamauga-Chattanooga National Military Park. (hs)

Signal Point Park is a unit of the CCNMP. A foot trail here leads down to a couple of different overlooks, each of which presents a view of the Tennessee River Gorge, below, and of Raccoon Mountain directly across the river. From here, the historically minded traveler can gain a great appreciation for the terrain difficulties the Union army faced in re-supplying itself in Chattanooga. The name derives from the Union signal station that was positioned here, used in relaying communications between Bridgeport and Chattanooga, connecting the Federal army to the outside world.

To Tour Stop 3

Return to US 127. Exit the park, turn right onto James Blvd., and then bear left onto Mississippi Ave. Once at Signal Mountain Blvd., turn right. At US 127, again turn right and head back down the mountain.

In 3.0 miles, turn right onto TN highway 27 West (also known as the Cherokee Trail and Suck Creek Road. Yes, it is confusing). Follow TN 27 W for 14.5 miles. When you reach the intersection of TN 27 and TN 283, pause.

GPS: N 35.18946, W 85.48603

At Powell's Crossroads

Though adorned with modern trappings, Powell's Crossroads is still a sleepy, peaceful small town in Sequatchie Valley. The Cumberland Plateau looms in the distance. (hs)

At least part of the time, you will be following one of the various supply routes used between Bridgeport and Chattanooga. That portion of the road along the Tennessee River was known as Haley's Trace. That route was closed to Union wagons in early October 1863 when Confederate sharpshooters, firing from across the river, were able to pick off mules and teamsters at will.

As you climb Walden's Ridge along TN 27 at Suck Creek, you leave the historic road. TN 27 breaks off to the west to descend Walden's Ridge through Kernel's Gap, but no usable wagon road ran through here in 1863.

Once you reach the intersection of TN 283 in the town of Powell's Crossroads, you are in the middle of the Sequatchie Valley, astride the main road to Bridgeport, which lies to your left. Before we head that way, however, we are going farther north, to the site of Anderson's Crossroads.

→**To Tour Stop 4**

Turn right onto TN 283 N, which is also known as the Alvin C. York Highway or the East Valley Rd. Travel

*approximately 6.75 miles north to the intersection of 283
and Frank Tate Rd. Find a safe place to stop here.*

GPS: N 35.27410, W 85.42884

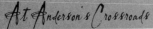

Here the East Valley Road crosses Anderson's Mill Creek, just south of Anderson's Crossroads. (hs)

In 1863, this was the location of Anderson's
Crossroads. A short distance south of here, you
drove over Anderson's Mill Creek. Anderson's Mill
was off to your east, at the foot of Walden's Ridge,
while the Anderson house sat just north of the
mill. The old road came down through Anderson's
Gap, off to your northeast, and then zig-zagged
down the mountain to this location. On October
2, 1863, Wheeler's Confederate cavalry attacked
a Union supply train here, which Wheeler
estimated as 10 miles long and containing 800-
1,500 wagons. Much of the train had turned and
was already headed up the mountain. Virtually all
the wagons were captured and ransacked, then
burned, hundreds of mules were slaughtered,
and perhaps 1,500 Federals were paroled. Union
General Rosecrans later reported that only 300
army wagons were lost, which was probably as
much an understatement as Wheeler's reported
figure was an over-estimate. One reason for the
discrepancy was the inclusion of a large number

of private wagons, owned by sutlers and the like, accompanying the official army train for safety. In any case, the loss of the train dealt a severe blow to Union logistical capacity in besieged Chattanooga.

➤ To Tour Stop 5

Turn around and head back south on TN 283 until you reach the intersection at Powell's Crossroads. Turn right here, and continue to follow TN 283 until it ends at TN 28. Turn left on TN 28 S and proceed 11.2 miles to I-24. Enter I-24 west to Exit 152 A, US Highway 72 South. In 5 miles, exit US 72 onto Alabama 277, turning left at the ramp. In 2.6 miles, turn left onto 7th St. in Bridgeport. Watch for and follow the signs to the Bridgeport Train Depot Museum.

The Train Depot Museum has limited hours, so some prior planning is required if you wish to view the museum.

GPS: N 34.94864, W 85.71116

Bridgeport's historic (if postwar) train depot now houses the Bridgeport Historical Society. (hs)

Bridgeport was the end of the Union rail line in 1863, although it was not the Federal army's main supply depot. That was at Stevenson, Alabama, because there was no way to turn trains around at Bridgeport, and so any train that came this far had to back up all the way to Stevenson in order to reverse order and head back to Nashville. Most trains stopped and unloaded at Stevenson.

The railroad bridge that gave Bridgeport its name was destroyed by the retreating Confederates in July 1863, and though the Union army had already arranged for it to be rebuilt, construction was delayed as long as those same Confederates besieged Chattanooga. General Howard established his headquarters here, with Union pontoon bridges supporting a bridgehead on the south bank of the Tennessee.

The depot building dates from 1917.

➤ To Tour Stop 6

Drive back to 7th St. and turn left. At Alabama Rte. 277, turn left and head south. In approximately 9 miles, you will reach Stevenson (AL 277 is called 2nd St. in town). At Kentucky Ave. (also known as AL 117), turn right. At Main St., turn left, and park by the Railroad Depot Museum.

Like the museum in Bridgeport, hours are seasonal and limited: plan your trip before you go.

GPS: N 34.86765, W 85.83973

At Stevenson—The Depot, Fort Harker, and "The little Brick"

Stevenson was a major hub of Union activity in 1863. The current depot building dates from 1872 and now serves as a museum. It stands on the site of the 1852 depot building. Across the street stood a hotel and commercial buildings. The museum now houses displays on local history and on the Civil War.

Due to its importance as a forward supply base, Stevenson was also heavily fortified. Its defenses included two forts, some smaller redoubts, and several blockhouses all placed to defend the depot and the local railroad infrastructure. Of those, one structure remains: Fort Harker, several blocks away on Sawmill St. In its recreated form, Fort Harker as viewed today represents the fort it was in 1864, when it was named for Union Brig. Gen. Charles G. Harker, killed at the battle of Kennesaw Mountain. However, the first Union fortification here was erected in 1862, subsequently abandoned, and then considerably strengthened in 1863 when Stevenson became the supply head for General Rosecrans's campaign to capture Chattanooga.

In 1863 the Union army depended on the railroad to transport supplies to the forces in the field—track that stretched back to Nashville,

Stevenson's historic depot now houses an interesting museum devoted to Stevenson's history, including exhibits on both railroading and the Civil War. (hs)

and ultimately, Louisville, Kentucky. Because the railroad was vulnerable to attack by Rebel cavalry and partisans, that supply line was frequently interrupted. Stockpiling supplies at forward bases like Stevenson became critical to keeping the army operating effectively while those interruptions were dealt with. Thus, Stevenson was filled with such supplies. Huge piles of crates and barrels, livestock corrals, and a not-insignificant tent city for the Federal garrison filled every available open space.

A few blocks east of the Depot, on Myrtle Street, can be found the ruins of a brick house that was once the headquarters of the Union garrison. This building, known as "the Little Brick," served as a headquarters for William Rosecrans, Joseph Hooker, and other Union officers while in town.

Despite its modest, small-town air today, in 1863 Stevenson was one of the most important places in the region; activity of all kinds swarmed here, night and day.

To Tour Stop 7

From the Depot Museum, retrace your steps to AL 277 (2nd St.) and take that north to US 72. Take the ramp for US 72 North, returning to US Interstate Highway 24. In 13 miles, take the ramp for I-24 East. In 9 miles, you will take exit 161, TN Highway 156, and turn left at the bottom of the ramp. Travel 0.5 miles until you reach the intersection with TN 134. Turn right and proceed 2 miles. On the right side of the road, after you pass Parker Ln, but before you travel under the modern railroad bridge, you should see a Civil War Trails Marker on the right of the road. Pull over here.

GPS: N 35.00283, W 85.51185

At Running Water Creek

In 1863, the Union army had to rebuild this large trestle bridge before rail communications could be restored into Chattanooga. This bridge was an engineering challenge second only to the bridge over the Tennesse River at Bridgeport. (hs)

This bridge was also destroyed in July 1863 by the Confederate Army of Tennessee. Like the bridge over the Tennessee River, rebuilding the bridge here was crucial to long-term Union planning. Chattanooga was intended to be the next major supply base, for what ultimately would be the campaign to take Atlanta. If that were to happen, then Chattanooga's rail connections to the outside world had to be re-established. Before those repairs could begin, the Federal army needed to regain control of Lookout Valley.

The small community ahead, just past the railroad bridge, is called Whiteside. Major General Joseph Hooker's combined XI and XII Corps troops marched into this narrow valley on October 27, skirmishing with a handful of Confederate cavalry as they did so. The XI Corps camped at Whiteside that night. The next day they pushed on to Brown's Ferry and Wauhatchie.

To return to I-24, turn around. Travel west on TN 134 back to TN 156 and turn left. The Interstate is ahead.

➤ To Tour 2

If you wish to continue to Wauhatchie for Tour 2, continue east on TN 134 until it crosses into Georgia, where it becomes GA Rte. 299. Proceed for 6 miles until you come to the junction with US Highway 11. Turn left onto US 11 North, which will take you back to I-24 and to Wauhatchie.

GPS: N 35.01533, W 85.37524

The New York Peace Memorial, the largest monument on the Chattanooga battlefield, was dedicated on November 1, 1910. Sculptor Hinton Perry produced the bronze figures that stand atop the 85-foot-tall monument, which cost more than $100,000. (cm)

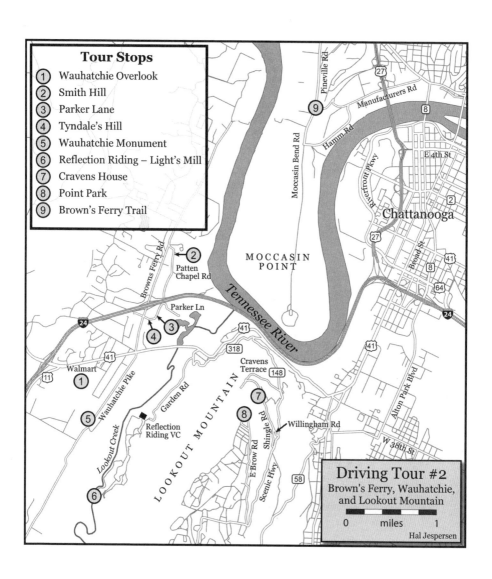

Tour Stops

1. Wauhatchie Overlook
2. Smith Hill
3. Parker Lane
4. Tyndale's Hill
5. Wauhatchie Monument
6. Reflection Riding – Light's Mill
7. Cravens House
8. Point Park
9. Brown's Ferry Trail

Pineville Rd

27

Manufacturers Rd

8

Hamm Rd

E 4th St

Moccasin Bend Rd

Riverfront Pkwy

Chattanooga

Browns Ferry Rd

2

Patten
Chapel Rd

MOCCASIN
POINT

27

2

Broad St

41

8

Parker Ln

3

Tennessee River

64

4

24

41

318

24

Walmart

41

Cravens
Terrace

148

41

11

1

7

Wauhatchie Pike

Garden Rd

318

8

Alton Park Blvd

5

Reflection
Riding VC

Willingham Rd

W 38th St

Lookout Creek

LOOKOUT MOUNTAIN

E Brow Rd

Scenic Hwy

58

6

Driving Tour #2
Brown's Ferry, Wauhatchie,
and Lookout Mountain

0   miles   1

Hal Jespersen

Brown's Ferry, Wauhatchie, and Lookout Mountain

DRIVING TOUR 2

⟶ **To Tour Stop 1**

This tour begins at exit 174 of Interstate (I-24.) From whichever direction you approach, exit into US Highway 41 north, which almost immediately also becomes US 11 N. You will see the signs to the Walmart supercenter on the right. Turn right and go up the hill into the parking lot. Drive past the store to the left end of the lot (as you face the building) where you will find yourself on the edge of a hill overlooking the valley below.

A Walmart might seem like a strange place to begin a tour, but the location provides the most expansive vista of the Wauhatchie battlefield.

GPS: N 35.01533, W 85.37524

At Wauhatchie Overlook (Walmart parking lot)

The small neighborhood seen below covers the north end of the Wauhatchie battlefield. Bratton's South Carolina brigade advanced southeast (from your left to your right) toward the industrial park farther to your right. Those industrial buildings mark the Union positions. There is a small monument there that we will visit later.

The road bordering the far end of the neighborhood is the modern Wauhatchie Pike, with the railroad paralleling it just beyond. Beyond that,

The modern historian takes those vantage points he can find, however unexpected. The Walmart's parking lot offers a spectacular view of the Wauhatchie Battlefield from above. Lookout is to the left. (hs)

of course, rises Lookout Mountain. On a clear day the view is impressive. On other days, the fog can be so thick it is sometimes impossible to see even the houses spread out below.

Bratton's brigade was deployed on this side of the Pike and Railroad, though two Confederate regiments attempted to work around the Union right flank via the far side of the road.

To your right, looking northeast, you can see the line of hills marking the Confederate positions of Benning's, Robertson's, and Law's brigades lining the east side of the Wauhatchie Pike north of US 41 and 11. Those hills are where the Union XI Corps engaged on the night of October 29. We will go there next.

(Driving note: Brown's Ferry Rd., which we are about to take, does indeed lead to Brown's Ferry, but even though the Civil War Trust acquired some land at Brown's Ferry, as of this writing, it is not yet accessible to visitors. At the end of this tour, there are directions on how to find Brown's Ferry from the Moccasin Bend side of the Tennessee River.)

→ **To Tour Stop 2**

Exit the Walmart parking lot and turn right. Travel 0.7 miles to the intersection of US 41/11, Wauhatchie Pike, and Brown's Ferry Rd. Turn left onto Brown's Ferry Rd. Travel 1.9 miles to the intersection of Patten Chapel Rd. on

*your right. Turn right. The road curves around, and you will
come to the Lookout Valley Presbyterian Church. Pull over
here or find a safe place to park. Look across the road to the
hills on your left.*

GPS: N 35.03572, W 85.35854

Smith Hill

You are now facing the north end of the hill
complex stormed by Smith's Brigade of the XI Corps
on the night of October 29, 1863. The hill directly to
the front was partially occupied by the 4th Texas, with
Law's five Alabama regiments extending southward
and then the 3rd Arkansas on the other flank.

The 136th New York moved around this hill
to the north, advancing to the river bank and then
turning south, which is where Sgt. Val Giles of the
4th Texas was captured. Farther to the south, the 33rd
Massachusetts and 73rd Ohio charged up the face of
the hill there to eventually collapse Law's Alabamians.

The next stop will take you close to the south end
of this hill complex. As you drive south along Patten
Chapel Rd., take note of the terrain. As the road
bends slightly to the right, you are opposite the Hill
complex's saddle, and at the approximate site of the
33rd Massachusetts's position.

➤ To Tour Stop 3

*Drive south along Patten Chapel Rd. until it makes a
90-degree right turn, with the I-24 Expressway just ahead.
You will come back out onto Brown's Ferry Rd., turn left and
pass under I-24. The next left after the expressway ramps will
be Parker Ln. Turn left here. You should see a McDonald's
south of the lane and a Comfort Suites Hotel on the north side
of the street.*

*Parker Ln. curves behind the modern development and
joins up with what was the Chattanooga Rd. in 1863. That
lane leads to what is now park property, but almost immediately
you will see a locked gate.*

*Due to the remote nature of the park property along Parker
Ln., for security and safety reasons, this gate is usually locked.
Intrepid souls may proceed farther on foot, but be careful of
leaving your vehicle unattended. It is approximately a 1-mile
walk to the end of Parker Ln., for a 2-mile round trip.*

GPS: N 35.02638, W 85.36156

At Parker Lane

The gate at Parker Lane. Today, the park service restricts vehicle acess to Parker Ln. due to safety and security concerns. (hs)

First take note of the hills around you. The hill directly behind and south of the McDonald's Restaurant is Tyndale Hill, where Benning's Georgians were stationed and which Tyndale's brigade was ordered to capture.

Going north, if you were to walk along Parker Ln. until it curves abruptly to the right, you will come across a monument to the New York regiments in the XI Corps, sometimes called the "Von Steinwehr Monument." In fact, it commemorates the New York regiments in both Schurz's and Steinwehr's commands. (Alert drivers heading east along I-24 can see this monument from the highway.) The monument sits at the southern end of the Smith Hill complex, in the approximate position of the 3rd Arkansas Infantry.

Parker Ln. ends at a small family cemetery, called Fryar Cemetery, another half-mile to the east. Just beyond Fryar Cemetery you can walk out into the open clearing of an overhead power line, a clearing from where you will have a fine view of both Lookout Creek and Lookout Mountain. This is the same perspective shown in James Walker's paintings of the battle.

A view of the Von Steinwehr New York Monument from Parker Ln. The interstate highway lies just beyond the large pine tree in the background. (hs)

⟶ To Tour Stop 4

Once back at your vehicle, head back toward Brown's Ferry Rd. Just before you pass the McDonald's restaurant on your left, you will see a small side lane, called Drew St. If you can, pause here.

GPS: N 35.02541, W 85.36315

At Tyndale's Hill

The hill you see to your southeast is Tyndale's Hill. It was occupied first by a regiment of Bratton's South Carolina brigade, then Benning's Georgia brigade, and finally, Hector Tyndale's brigade of Schurz's division, the XI Corps. There is no public access to Tyndale's Hill today.

⟶ To Tour Stop 5

Return to Brown's Ferry Rd. and turn left, heading south. Cross US Hwy 11, continuing straight. The street is now called Wauhatchie Pike. Proceed another 0.9 miles until you see a monument on your right. Find a safe place to pull over and stop here.

GPS: N 35.00963, W 85.37446

At Wauhatchie Monument

The Wauhatchie monument, again to the New York Regiments in Geary's division. The knoll where Knap's Battery was positioned now holds the building to the right. The rail line runs just out of sight to the left. (hs)

This marker is dedicated to Brig. Gen. George Sears Greene's 3rd Brigade, Geary's division, of the XII Corps. The rise of ground where the office now sets just to the southwest marks the knoll where Knapp's battery was engaged on the night of October 28th–29th, 1863. If you stand and face the monument, Greene's men were deployed in an arc, running west from this position and south along the railroad embankment behind you. Bratton's South Carolinians approached from the north (your right) with the 6th South Carolina astride the road, then the 1st, 5th, and Hampton's Legion extending west, while the 2nd South Carolina Rifles and the Palmetto Legion Sharpshooters maneuvered to turn Greene's flank east of the railroad.

Note: from Greene's Monument, if it were possible to head due east you would strike Lookout Creek, and soon reach the site of Light's Mill, where a month after the Wauhatchie fight, Geary's division, reinforced by Brig. Gen. Whitaker's brigade of the IV Corps, crossed Lookout Creek to assail the Confederates on the slopes of Lookout Mountain. Unfortunately, no public access leads to Light's Mill from this direction, so we must come at it another way.

⟶ To Tour Stop 6

Head back north on Wauhatchie Pike. Return to US 11 and turn right. Travel 0.7 miles and turn right onto the Old Wauhatchie Pike, also known as TN Rte. 318. The next right (0.1 miles) will be Garden Rd. A historical marker denotes the battle of Lookout Mountain on your right, at the intersection with Garden Rd.

Turn right and follow Garden Rd. to the Reflection Riding Arboretum and Nature Center. This is not National Park Land, and there will be an entrance fee. The Center will take you to the site of Light's Mill, however, and traverse open ground that witnessed the Union advance during the early stages of the battle of Lookout Mountain. Follow the driving route through the center to the site of the millstones in the very southwest corner. Along the way, you will notice a couple of markers that mention the battle.

GPS: N 35.00769, W 85.36660

The intersection of the Old Wauhatchie Pike and Garden Road. The historical marker to the right denotes the battle of Lookout Mountain. (hs)

As you enter Reflection Riding Arboretum and Nature Center, you are south of the wartime Confederate picket line and will be driving along terrain covered mostly by the Federals of Colonel Candy's brigade. Ireland's and Cobham's brigades moved north on the slopes above the nature center, negotiating the more difficult terrain of Lookout's rugged lower shoulder.

This sign describes the millstones of Light's Mill, which stood just to the left and on the other side of Lookout Creek. (hs)

At the millstones, stop and exit your vehicle. According to the nature center, these stones were from Light's Mill, which originally sat on the opposite bank of Lookout Creek, just a bit south of your current location. Light's Mill is named for its owner, Michael Light, who acquired the mill in the 1830s after the Cherokee Removal. (See page 87 for photo; GPS: N 34.99812 W 85.37330)

Geary's Federals fashioned a crossing here at Light's Mill. The construction and subsequent deployment consumed much of the morning of November 24. Fog largely concealed this Union activity. Geary's battle line ran from here eastward up the slope of the mountain to the palisade, facing north. Whitaker's brigade, of the IV Corps, formed in two lines behind Geary near the palisade.

→ **To Tour Stop 7**

Exit Reflection Riding Arboretum and Nature Center and return to TN Rte. 318, the Old Wauhatchie Pike. Turn right here. Follow the Old Wauhatchie Pike for 0.9 miles until you come to the intersection of TN Rte. 148, also known as Scenic Highway. Turn right here. Follow TN Rte. 148 for 1.2 miles, until you come to Willingham Rd. – also known as Linear Rd. (Note, look for the brown informational sign pointing you to the Cravens House.) Turn right here. At the next right, turn right onto Shingle Rd.

In 0.5 miles, you will come to a small parking lot on your left. Park here and exit the vehicle.

GPS: N 35.01365, W 85.34176

At Cravens House

The Cravens House today. Lt. Gibson's two Confederate artillery pieces sit in the foreground, with Chattanooga off in the distnace. (dp)

You will see before you the Cravens House, a postwar structure that Thomas Cravens built in 1867 after the original was destroyed in the fighting. You will also see a number of monuments to various Federal regiments, as well as a number of War Department Tablets (the red and blue metal plaques) describing the fighting around the Cravens House. There is plenty to explore here. Visitors should walk the short trail (about 0.4 miles) to the Confederate entrenchments, which are really piled stone fortifications. The walk provides a good sense of the difficult nature of the terrain on either side of the trail.

Take note of the entrenchments, which are oriented to face west, down the slope of the mountain, rather than south, from where the Federals first approached. Here was where the first serious contact between Geary's men (Cobham's and Ireland's brigades) and Walthall's Mississippi troops occurred. Outflanked from the right and behind (above), the Mississippians were forced to retreat.

It will take some time to view all the monuments and tablets here, but a close reading of the tablets helps to understand the flow of the battle. There are several markers up the hill overlooking the Cravens House plateau, as well as a series of Confederate tablets back along the road toward TN Rte. 148.

If you want to visit the large Iowa Monument on the shelf below the Cravens House, you can either walk (a bit of a climb) or drive: simply go back out of the parking lot along Cravens Terrace until you come to Military Dr. (just a few yards), turn left, go one block, and turn left again onto Caroline St.

Once you are finished exploring the Cravens House, we will conclude our driving tour at Point Park.

➤ To Tour Stop 8

Return to TN Rte. 148, Scenic Highway, and turn right. Follow TN 148 for 1.4 miles to Bragg Ave. Turn right again. In 0.9 miles, turn left onto East Brow Rd. In 0.2 miles, East Brow ends at Point Rd. The Lookout Mountain Battlefield Visitor Center is on your left, with Point Park on your right. You can choose between street parking or a small NPS public lot next to the Visitor Center. There is a small fee to visit Point Park.

GPS: N 35.00969, W 85.34389

At Point Park

Though very little significant fighting occurred here, the view from the top of Lookout Mountain has made it one of the premier tourist destinations in the Chattanooga region, something that was equally true in 1863. Many thousands of soldiers, both Union and Confederate, trooped up to the top of the mountain. It was a popular spot for photographs, especially at iconic Umbrella Rock. Today, Point Park has walking trails and viewing platforms, including the Ochs observatory and museum.

The Visitor Center also houses the restored James Walker canvas, *The Battle of Lookout Mountain*, the massive 13 x 30 foot painting depicting the battle and—most prominently—General Joseph Hooker's role in the engagement.

This concludes the main driving tour.

The National Park Service's visitor center atop Lookout Mountain, on the left, sits near the castle-like entrance to the ten-acre Point Park. The park, which does charge an admission fee, offers a panoramic view of Chattanooga. (hs)

Those who wish may also explore Brown's Ferry from the Moccasin Bend side of the Tennessee River:

From US Interstate 24, traveling either east or west, take the ramp to US 27 north at exit 178. Travel 3.5 miles on US 27 N. Cross the river and immediately exit at Manufacturers Rd. At the bottom of the ramp, turn left. Follow Manufacturers Rd. until it ends at Pineville Rd. Manufacturers Rd. will split into a Y intersection just before you reach Pineville Rd., bear left, and once at the intersection of Pineville Rd., you will see a small parking lot for the Brown's Ferry Federal Rd. NPS Trail across the street. Park there.

GPS: N 35.05855, W 85.33121

The Brown's Ferry trail follows part of the route of the old Federal Rd. It is a 1.2-mile round trip to the banks of the Tennessee River, opposite Brown's Ferry, where an interpretive marker points out the exact site.

The Brown's Ferry Trailhead on Moccasin Bend. In addition to its Civil War Significance, Brown's Ferry played a major role in the Cherokee Removal of the 1830s (the Trail of Tears) and was the site of the Federal Road connecting Chattanooga with the rest of Tennessee. (hs)

At Moccasin Bend

1. Brown's Ferry Trail

This trail follows much of the original Federal Rd., down which passed many of the troops and pontoons that were used to complete the bridge over the Tennessee once Hazen's brigade had landed on the opposite shore. The Federal Rd. here was also part of the Cracker Line running into Chattanooga after the Union army cleared Lookout Valley of Confederates.

The trail to Brown's Ferry begins next to the parking area. The nearby sign offers a trail map to help orient visitors. (hs)

2. Union Artillery positions

Though the Union artillery positions on Moccasin Bend are not far from the Brown's Ferry Trail, currently there is no established walking trail to those positions. They are on NPS land, however, and can be accessed by more adventurous visitors. Due to a lack of parking and the proximity of non-public land, please inquire at the desk at either Visitor Center about the best way to access these positions.

The Myth of the Cracker Line

APPENDIX A

BY FRANK VARNEY

If you look in pretty much any history of the Civil War that discusses the siege of Chattanooga, you will find some assertion that General William S. Rosecrans, commander of the Army of the Cumberland, after his defeat at Chickamauga went into a state of depression that essentially destroyed his capacity for command. From an intelligent, aggressive commander, he supposedly turned into a dazed wreck—his confidence shattered, his spirit broken, he became unable to take even the most basic steps to keep his army supplied and in fighting trim. It required Ulysses S. Grant, who was appointed to overall command of Union forces in the region, to save Rosecrans's army. Grant relieved Rosecrans, replaced him with George H. Thomas, and promptly set about devising a remarkably clear plan for getting the supplies flowing. The energy and resourcefulness of Grant resulted in the opening of the Cracker Line in an incredibly short time, which saved the Army of the Cumberland. This is often, in fact, considered one of his more noteworthy accomplishments.

A closer examination of the primary sources, however, reveals much more to the story. The questions that must therefore be asked are simple: was Army of the Cumberland starving and did Grant rescue it from oblivion?

According to military historian J. F. C. Fuller, "within five days of Grant's arrival in Chattanooga, the road to Bridgeport was opened, and within a week the troops were receiving full rations . . . and a cheerfulness prevailed not before enjoyed in many weeks. Neither officers nor men looked upon themselves any longer as doomed." Fuller's source—and the source for the quote he uses to strengthen his statement—is Grant's memoirs.

Similarly, Ernest and Trevor Dupuy say that Grant "arrived at Chattanooga on [October 23rd]. Then things began to happen. In a few days food was abundant, worn-out clothing and equipment had been replaced, and the meager store of ammunition had been replenished. The Army of the Cumberland was ready to fight again." The Dupuys provide no source for this statement, but it sounds remarkably similar to what Fuller said—and Fuller's source was Grant himself.

The Cracker Line got its name from the hardtack, or crackers, that made up the core of a soldier's rations.

Popular historian Robert Leckie says, "The situation could hardly have been worse, and for Grant, whose spirit thrived on adversity, that was tantamount to never being better. Almost at once he determined to open a supply line. Thus was opened the famous 'cracker line' over which troops and supplies came into Chattanooga."

Geoffrey Perret does not give Grant all the credit but does accept the idea that the Army of the Cumberland was in danger of starving—although he gives no source for that statement. William B. Feis claims that "Rosecrans faced a severe shortage of supplies and nerve" and that Grant opened "the famous 'Cracker Line,' which helped alleviate some of the suffering." Feis, too, cites Grant as his source.

Jean Edward Smith says, "For Grant, the initial task was to reestablish a viable supply route . . . what he called 'a cracker line.'" And, although Smith acknowledges that the plan had been designed before Grant's arrival, he credits George H. Thomas and "Baldy" Smith, not Rosecrans. His source, once again, is Grant.

Ample evidence demonstrates that the Army of the Cumberland suffered supply problems caused mainly by the activity of Rebel cavalry, which continually cut the few available roads into Chattanooga, and by the terrible condition of the roads, exacerbated by miserable weather. Long before the campaign even began, Rosecrans predicted trouble if his mounted arm were not strengthened to counteract the Rebel horsemen, and his predictions came true; nor did his entreaties for more cavalry end with Chickamauga. He sent messages to General in Chief Henry Halleck on October 1 and 2 and to Secretary of War Edwin Stanton six days later on that subject.

Evidence also exists, however, that conditions were not as bad as they have often been represented. In the archives at Stones River and Chickamauga-Chattanooga National Battlefields, hundreds of copies of letters and dozens of journals written by men present in Chattanooga during the siege are available for review. Remarkably few of these documents record any serious shortage of food, although many complain of the monotony of the diet.

A commonly quoted witness reported seeing men following supply wagons and picking up dried corn that had spilled from them. The implication is that hungry men were scavenging food to fill their empty bellies, but it is at least as likely that they were trying to find fodder for their starving animals. Although the horses and mules were suffering terribly due to a lack of forage, the men—while in some cases on severely reduced rations—seem to have been in no imminent danger of starvation. In fact, some of them said that they were eating fairly well. Consider the following journal entry from October 5: "We got some potatoes, apples, etc. . . . the country in which we were to forage contained plenty and we did not want for meat etc."

Baldy Smith proved a capable-enough commander on the battlefield, but his tendency to talk too much landed him in trouble time and time again. Rescued from obscurity by Grant, Smith would find himself by mid-1864 at the head of a corps in the Army of the James, where he would repay Grant's faith by again squabbling too much with other generals. Grant would eventually relieve him. (loc)

However, the reports of Assistant Secretary of War Charles Dana, designed to injure Rosecrans and establish a case for his removal, deliberately emphasized the shortages. Rosecrans, in attempting to convince Halleck that he needed assistance, may also have overstated the difficulties. And, Grant certainly misrepresented the situation after the fact. Grant said in his memoirs that the army was in a sorry state when he arrived in Chattanooga: starving, shoeless, with no fuel for cooking or heating, and in a terrible state of morale. Rosecrans took great offense at these statements, responding emphatically that "[w]hen I left it . . . the Army of the Cumberland was in no such condition."

Rosecrans went on to say that there was fuel in abundance, and that "[t]eams were hauling and delivering rations." He took particular note of the fact that Grant's famous message to Thomas directing that Chattanooga be held at all costs—sent when Grant assumed overall command and relieved Rosecrans—was the source of great annoyance to both Thomas and Rosecrans, neither of whom had any intention of doing otherwise.

In his memoirs, Grant gave Thomas's oft-quoted reply—"We shall hold the town until we starve"—but did not give the rest of the sentence: "our wagons are hauling rations from Bridgeport." Thomas went on to add, "204,462 rations in storehouses, 90,000 to arrive tomorrow." That certainly seems to indicate both that the Army of the Cumberland was not on the brink of starvation—not with more than 200,000 rations in Chattanooga (enough for approximately five days)—and with enough for two more on the way. Historians have repeatedly accepted Grant's version of this exchange, to the point that the abridged version is probably one of the most famous quotations of the war. Unfortunately, the rest of Thomas's statement is ignored.

A journal kept by one soldier had the following notations. On October 10, he reported the men were in possession of "chickens and vegetables . . . fresh pork and mutton also." The next day he noted, "forage is abundant. . . . The boys have attacked a lot of hogs and skirmishing is brisk, so I must put on the pot as I smell fresh pork." On October 17, he wrote of confiscating "nine barrels of sorghum molasses . . . also 60 bushels of sweet potatoes." On October 18, he reported, "We are now living on sweet potatoes." He noted a shortage of hardtack and meat, but there is little or no evidence in his journal of true hardship.

Division commander Philip H. Sheridan said that he was able to obtain "large quantities of corn for my animals and food for the officers and men. [I]n this way I carried men and animals through our beleaguerment in pretty fair condition."

It certainly appears that some units suffered less than others. No doubt some in the Army of the Cumberland felt hunger, but it was far from universal. What hunger existed cannot be solely attributed to any error of Rosecrans; and even if Grant had not relieved Rosecrans, it likely would have been ended in short order.

Nor did Quartermaster General Montgomery Meigs, sent to Chattanooga to discern the truth about conditions there, find that the army was in dire straits. According to a newspaper report, he disagreed with "the opinions expressed by arrivals from the army, that it was disheartened, demoralized, &c. On the contrary, he declares that it is in excellent condition and fully equal for any emergency." More tellingly, on September 27, he informed Stanton that he had found the men to be "vigorous, hearty, cheerful, and confident." Of the defenses, he noted that "the position is very strong already, and rapidly approaching a perfect security against assault. Nothing but a regular siege could, I think, reduce it. When the river rises the bridges will go, but the river will become navigable. One steam-boat and a few flats are ready for service. Another steam-boat is nearing completion. For another the machinery is at Bridgeport."

This certainly sounds as though Rosecrans and his staff were making energetic efforts to improve things. "When the troops understood to be on their way here arrive, General Rosecrans expects to recover command of the river to Bridgeport. Supplies can then be accumulated by water."

Of course, Rosecrans did not get the chance; Grant arrived just ahead of those troops, admirably completed what remained to be done, and got the credit for having done it all. "[A]nimals still in very fair condition, so far as I have seen them," Grant reported. "Plenty of them here and at Nashville." That does not sound as though the situation at that time—only a few weeks before Rosecrans's removal—was critical or even nearing that point.

It is worth noting that one of Fuller's criticisms of Rosecrans was that he "made no effort to run boats down the river. There were two at Chattanooga, and these could have brought 200 tons of supplies daily." According to Meigs, however, the reason Rosecrans did not use them was because the river was not yet deep enough to navigate. By the time it was, Rosecrans was gone.

Of the railroad connection from Nashville, Meigs commented, "The iron is reported on the ground; all but 4 miles graded." His final judgment was that "[t]hings look much better here than I expected to find them when I left Nashville; still success will demand efforts from the army and from the country. Of the rugged nature of this region, I had no conception when I left Washington. I never traveled on such roads before." On October 1, Meigs told Stanton, "This army is most ready, and laborious as well as courageous. It builds its own bridges, makes pontoons, and lives within itself. It is in many respects most admirable." Again, this is not a picture of a beaten and demoralized army, starving and lacking faith in its general.

In his *Personal Memoirs*, Grant noted that Rosecrans's chief of engineers (Gen. William F.

"Baldy" Smith) had put a sawmill into operation, had one bridge completed, was well on his way to constructing another, was assembling materials for a third, and had an ingeniously improvised steamer in operation on the river—but he stated it in such a way as to make it appear that the officer had done it entirely on his own. There is no hint of credit attributed to Rosecrans for these accomplishments even though they had, of course, been achieved while he commanded the army. Rosecrans, not Smith, ordered their implementation.

Grant also commented that Rosecrans had "excellent" plans in place to establish an efficient supply line, and "my only wonder was that he had not carried them out." William McFeely says that Rosecrans "had many intelligent suggestions about how the army should proceed, and Grant could only wonder why Rosecrans had not himself put them into effect." If that sounds familiar, it is because McFeely's source is again, Grant. In fact, implementation had already begun. Rosecrans had issued orders to take all necessary steps to improve the line of communications, as may be plainly seen in the *Official Records* (*OR*) by anyone willing to take the time to make a close study of them rather than merely relying upon the writings of Grant.

However, there is yet another source that supports this position: the testimony of the soldiers in the ranks. On October 10, Sgt. Maj. Lyman Widney of the 34th Illinois recorded in his journal that conditions were expected to improve very soon since the supply line had been opened that same day and troops and batteries had been deployed to guard it. More interesting, however, is the entry for October 11, which states, "the cracker line is in working order." In fact, the first journal reference using the name "Cracker Line" is as early as October 5, and Widney used the term again on the 6th. At that point the line was not yet completely open, but given the fact that it was being referred to by name, it clearly was a project already in the works. According to Widney, supplies were flowing freely on the 11th.

This is a very significant document. Widney referred to the Cracker Line on October 5 as something that had been undertaken again on

October 6 as an ongoing project, and on October 10 as an open flow of supplies—more than a week before Rosecrans was relieved and nearly three weeks before Grant supposedly established the line that fed the Army of the Cumberland. Other letters and journals also make reference to the Cracker Line, and, although not all are dated, their context indicates that the line was opened prior to the relief of Rosecrans not after.

There is also the official record to consider. On October 10, Rosecrans received a message informing him that the depot in Nashville was "pushing forward cattle by land and railroad; shipped 200 to-day by railroad; am sending other stores also." On the 12th, Meigs informed Stanton that "I have given such orders and taken such steps during the seventeen days I have spent here as will, I think, much aid this army, and I do not think my presence here longer will be of much service."

On October 14, Rosecrans received a telegram from the War Department informing him that three million rations were en route if he could find a way to transport them from the railhead to Chattanooga. He replied that they should be sent as planned. If the supply system did actually collapse and hunger became a serious problem, it does not appear that it could have happened before, at the earliest, October 14 or so—not if the efficient, thorough, and well-regarded Meigs were telling us the truth. That means that any serious deficiency—assuming one ever existed—lasted only a handful of days and would have been addressed very quickly whether or not Rosecrans were relieved.

It is more probable that the purported "starvation" of the Army of the Cumberland is a myth. In a letter written October 18, Alfred L. Hough told his wife that due to a recent cavalry raid, "we are now short of rations." This implies that there was no shortage before. On October 20, the day Rosecrans was relieved, Hough wrote that the army had rations for another 12 days, warning only that "if the roads do not get better by that time" things *could* become dire.

Grant claimed that from his arrival in Chattanooga, it took him a week to open the supply line. In fact, the line was partially open nearly two weeks before he arrived. Grant did implement a plan to strengthen it, but that plan had been designed by Rosecrans, who had begun preparations for it. Even Philip Sheridan, second only to Sherman among the "Grant men," said that at the time the change of commanders took place, "Rosecrans was busy with preparations for a movement to open the direct road to Bridgeport." According to Sheridan, the arrival of Hooker and his men had given Rosecrans the resources he needed, and "[w]ith this force Rosecrans had already strengthened certain important points on the railroad . . . and given orders to Hooker to hold [his forces] in readiness to advance toward Chattanooga." Once Grant arrived, he "began at once to carry out the plans that had been formed for opening the . . . road to Bridgeport."

Shortly after the war, a great deal of controversy erupted over who should receive the acclaim for the plan. Historian Brooks Simpson, in his biography of Grant, wrote that "Rosecrans, Thomas, and [General William F.] Smith each claimed the honor for themselves. However, it was left to someone else to make sure that it was implemented." According to Simpson, Grant should get the credit for putting the plan into place because who designed it was moot. That seems logical, to a point. Of course, Rosecrans was about to implement his plan, Grant then relieved him; Thomas was the man in charge of the operation, even if Grant was in overall command; and Smith, though chief engineer of the Army of the Cumberland, did not have the authority to implement anything without the permission of his commanding officer. So, although Professor Simpson clearly thinks Grant should get the credit for putting into operation a plan someone else designed, approved, and implemented, that credit goes to Grant only by default.

In fact, no less an authority than George H. Thomas publicly placed the distinction where it belonged. When he ordered Hooker forward, Thomas told him to execute the movement "planned by General Rosecrans." In his report of the operations to secure Brown's Ferry and open Lookout Valley—operations for which Grant claimed credit and which are generally taken as the final act that secured the Cracker Line—Thomas opened by saying, "In pursuance of the plan of General Rosecrans, the execution of which had been deferred until Hooker's transportation [had arrived] . . . ." General Joseph Hooker said that the plan of the operation was "communicated to me by Rosecrans long before I ever saw Chattanooga."

Historian Geoffrey Perret, who seldom gives Rosecrans much credit, perceptively states that the plan "would have been implemented even if Rosecrans had not been fired." A court of inquiry convened in 1900 by then-Secretary of War Elihu Root took Hooker's statement into account when it found that "there is abundant evidence in the Official Records to show that the plan was devised and prepared by General Rosecrans." Of Grant's role in the operation, Rosecrans said that it "would have taken place all the same had he never lived."

Bruce Catton, one of the remarkably few historians not to give Grant all the credit for the "rescue" of Federal forces in Chattanooga, said that it was entirely possible the Federal troops would have broken the siege "even if Grant had never gone near Chattanooga." Grant's attempt to claim credit for this operation, as well as his attempt to claim credit for a victory at Chattanooga a few months later, Rosecrans later characterized as "insatiable and conscienceless egotism." Here Rosecrans may have gone too far. In his report to Halleck, Grant did acknowledge that the plan had been designed not by himself but by Smith and Thomas, but he still gave no credit to Rosecrans.

Once we examine the all primary source documents it becomes apparent that what we thought we knew about the Cracker Line needs to be rethought.

FRANK VARNEY is the author of *General Grant and the Rewriting of History: How the Destruction of General William S. Rosecrans Influenced Our Understanding of the Civil War*. A graduate of William Paterson University and Cornell University, he is an associate professor of US and Classical History at Dickinson State University.

A Tale of Two Paintings

APPENDIX B

Joseph Hooker's attack against the Confederates on Lookout Mountain may not have been the most decisive stroke of the campaign, but the feat's drama was unmatched. Given the topography, most of the men in both armies could view some part of the contest—at least when the fog and cloud cover allowed.

One of those watching wasn't a soldier at all. His name was James Walker, and he was an artist. By the 1860s, he was well known for work depicting scenes from the Mexican American War, including the large 8-by-17.5-foot *The Battle of Chapultepec*, commissioned for the newly constructed US Capitol building to hang in the Senate annex.

Why Walker was present in Chattanooga at the time of the battle remains a mystery. It is possible that he was there in connection with Union Gen. Montgomery C. Meigs. Meigs oversaw construction of the new capitol and commissioned much of the needed artwork. One such commission, in 1858, was Walker's enormous *Chapultepec* canvas, completed in 1862.

Another likely connection was with Theodore R. Davis, a "special artist" for *Harper's Weekly*. Davis's works appeared in many issues, and he accompanied Ulysses S. Grant at both Vicksburg and Chattanooga. Davis was also a student of Walker's. Born in 1840, Davis ventured to New York when he was fifteen, where he met and studied under Walker.

Whatever circumstances brought him there, Walker's presence in Chattanooga resulted in some of the more remarkable artwork of the war.

Walker was born an Englishman on June 3, 1819. His family emigrated to upstate New York when he was five years old, and they later moved to New York City. The source of his artistic training is obscure, even perhaps incomplete—some critics found his attempts at depicting the human form awkward and unrealistic.

Here, Park Ranger Lee White explains some of the finer details to be discerned in James Walker's monumental painting of the Battle of Lookout Mountain. (hs)

Walker drew this rough sketch prior to beginning work on his 1864 canvas on the battle. (loc)

He traveled to New Orleans as a young man, but his decision to travel to Mexico would have a deep impact on his career.

For a time he taught art at the Military College of Tampico. In 1847, he was living in Mexico City. The United States and Mexico were at war, but that conflict was remote, confined to the Rio Grande and Pacific coasts—at least until an American army landed at Veracruz and marched inland. With war now on his doorstep, some sources claim the Mexican government imprisoned Walker, while others claim he hid out in the city for six weeks. Once he was able, he left and joined the Americans, where army commander Winfield Scott put Walker's language skills to use as an interpreter. He was an eyewitness to much of the ensuing action, including the battle of Chapultepec on September 13, 1847.

After the Mexican War ended in 1848, Walker capitalized on his experiences, painting a series of twelve oil-on-board paintings about the conflict. Well received, their success garnered Walker a great deal of attention, allowing him to establish studios in New York and Washington—and eventually leading to the Chapultepec commission. By 1861, with a well-established reputation as a military artist, of course he set out to document the new conflict.

In 1864, the army commissioned Walker to paint a series of works depicting the fighting around Chattanooga. Not only was he an eyewitness to the Chattanooga battles, but he was afforded the

This is Walker's massive 1873 canvas, prepared at Hooker's direction. Joseph Hooker is at the forefront of Walker's work, drawing every eye. (nps)

opportunity to explore the terrain in detail as well as interview key participants such as Generals Thomas and Hooker.

He produced several canvasses, two of them battle scenes. The first was the *Battle of Chickamauga*, a work of oil on canvas, 13.5 inches by 40 inches, that depicted the timely arrival of Brig. Gen. James B. Steedman's division on Snodgrass Hill on September 20, 1863. The second was the *Battle of Lookout Mountain*. Another oil on canvas, this painting measured 14 by 40 inches—almost identical to the Chickamauga work—portraying the attack from General Hooker's perspective. He also completed a couple of less violent scenes focused on the mountain: one depicted a pair of Union officers descending the mountain after the battle. Another showed a detachment of Union cavalry moving along the road below the height's western face.

After the war, Walker returned to Washington and turned his attention to much larger canvasses. In conjunction with early Gettysburg historian John B. Bachelder, Walker completed the enormous 7.5-by-20-foot *Battle of Gettysburg*, portraying the repulse of Longstreet's July 3 assault.

In the meantime, the *Battle of Lookout Mountain* certainly caught Joseph Hooker's eye. The general was, after all, at the painting's center, mounted on his impressive white charger. But Hooker had something much more grandiose in mind—

more on the scale of *Gettysburg* or *Chapultepec*. He commissioned Walker to do a similar-sized version of the Lookout fight. Walker agreed.

The original painting had showed Hooker in the middle distance, directing an unlimbered artillery battery firing at the mountain. The foreground was dominated by the battery's limbers and by Hooker's mounted staff, waiting for action. While impressive, the scene was essentially static. Few figures showed any movement, and those doing so at no more than a walk. The mountain's bulk was the picture's primary focus.

The new work, aside from being far larger, leaves no doubt as to subject: Joe Hooker. Now General Hooker and his white steed are fully in the foreground, placed front and center. There is also much more movement: figures seem to pour onto the canvas from the right and left, with every line of the painting irresistibly drawing the viewer's focus to Hooker. Almost every figure depicted watches him. The mountain and surrounding hills, while still present, are subtly de-emphasized so as to not compete with the central image. Hooker was reputedly delighted with the result, valuing the work at $25,000—roughly $500,000 in 2016 dollars.

The painting went on exhibit in New York in the fall of 1874, though not everyone was equally enamored of it. In October 1874, one New York critic wrote:

> It was painted for Maj. Gen. Hooker, who, as we understand, in giving his order for the work requested that the battle might be represented as it was, and not as artists are in the habit of representing such subjects— by the introduction of incidents which never did and never could have occurred on any battlefield, or at least not on any of modern times. The General, in fact, (and he is supposed to know what a battle is like,) did not want gore for his money; neither did he desire to see clubbed muskets or brandished swords, or hand-to-hand fights,

Walker's 1864 work. Here the mountain itself dominates the scene. Hooker, while shown, is a much more distant figure than in the 1873 work. (usa)

or any of those little matters without which, according to the popular idea, a battle is no battle at all. . . .

Accordingly:

Mr. Walker was therefore desired to keep his canvas clear, and he has done so, but the effect it must be owned, is rather monotonous and disappointing . . . viewing it as a work of art, and such we presume it claims to be, we think it entitled to be termed respectable, but nothing more.

Some things never change.

This massive work quite possibly inspired Maj. Gen. Daniel Butterfield to commission a similar painting of the battle of Resaca, which was fought on May 14–15, 1864. Butterfield served under Hooker during the Atlanta campaign, both as Hooker's chief of staff and later as a divisional commander, and he was also a close personal friend. Butterfield was portrayed in Walker's Lookout Mountain opus as riding a black horse directly to Hooker's rear.

STORMING AND CAPTURE OF LOOKOUT MOUNTAIN,

Walker's was not the only painting to capture the drama of the "battle above the clouds." This lithograph clearly credits "Major General Joseph Hooker, commanding," although it did not feature him so prominently. (loc)

The fates of Walker's privately commissioned Lookout Mountain and Resaca paintings were convoluted, and each was almost lost to history, although the army-commissioned canvas became well known since it was accessible to the public. In the 1960s, the era of the Civil War centennial, it garnered a two-page spread in the wildly popular *American Heritage Picture History of the Civil War* as well as being used as a cover image for various other books, puzzles, and games. Millions of Americans saw it and remembered it.

The Hooker-commissioned work, by contrast, remained in family hands and out of sight for decades, suffering significant deterioration. It was finally donated to the National Park Service—with an appraised value of only $150, due to condition; the park service then raised the $100,000 needed to restore it. The painting was placed on permanent display at the Chickamauga & Chattanooga National Military Park's Point Park Visitor Center in 1986.

As a result, this painting has slowly superseded the earlier army-commissioned work in the public mind. With an overall annual Chickamauga-Chattanooga visitation of around one million people, hundreds of thousands of those visitors make the trek to Point Park and view the painting every year. Now that it is in the public domain, it has also become a common image for book jackets and other representations. In general, the viewing public (and this author) are far more impressed with the painting than was that long-ago New York art critic. It has a power and majesty that are very impressive when you come face to face with it.

And *Resaca?* This really was thought to be Walker's "lost work," rediscovered only recently. The painting originally hung in the New York National Guard's 12th Regiment Armory until that building was abandoned in 1958. All the artwork on display there, including Walker's *Resaca*, was shipped to the Brooklyn Navy yard for storage. Subsequently, the painting was sent to the West Point Military Academy Museum, and in the process, somehow

The Walker painting now hangs in the National Park Service visitor center just outside the entrance to Point Park atop Lookout Mountain. (hs)

got mislabeled as a copy of Walker's Gettysburg painting. In the 1970s, realizing that the painting belonged to the State of New York, West Point shipped it to the New York State Military Museum in Albany. There, still assuming it was only a copy of *Gettysburg*, it went back into storage. It wasn't until 2010, based on an inquiry from a man who owned an antique print of *Resaca*, that the museum realized that they had the original painting. As of this writing, the New York State Military Museum is still trying to determine how to display it properly, given the work's massive size.

Civil War Tourism: Lookout Mountain

APPENDIX C

Even though by 1863 the men of both the Union and Confederate armies were hardened veterans, seasoned by hard marching and bloody combat, they were also young men far from home—many for the first time ever. Caught up in what was likely to be the greatest adventure of their lives, they keenly observed everything around them. Despite war's horrors, they found time to gawk and sightsee, just like any other tourist away from home.

Lookout Mountain was considered one of the grandest sights of all. Famous even before the war as one of the more spectacular scenes in the new nation, it is hardly surprising that, as tens of thousands of soldiers converged on Chattanooga in the fall of 1863, Lookout became a well-visited place. In the many months between the end of fighting there in November 1863 and the beginning of the next campaign in the spring of 1864, many thousands of those men found the time to climb Lookout and take in the view.

Not surprisingly, as any tourist does, they also posed for photographs. Umbrella Rock, Hanging Rock, Pulpit Rock, Sunset Point and other photogenic points all served as backdrops for these images, taken by

"Group of 7th Illinois Soldiers on Lookout Mountain"—The Library of Congress cites the caption on the photograph, "with fuller name additions from the American Civil War Research Database" as: "1. R. L. Mountjoy [Robert L.], George Thompson, Geo. Sullivan [George], Israel P. Norris, Joseph Lancaster, Joel Decker, S. B. Hainline [Sylvester B.], John D. Gardner, M.V. Miller [Martin V.], Jesse Real, Co. D [Jesse T.], Edwin R. Jones. Wm. H. Kelly [William H. Kelley], L.D. Barnes [Lorenzo D.], Levi Allen, D.L. Allen [David L], Allen Hainline, Louis J. Allman [Lewis J.], John F. Hainline, John Q. Tompkins, Lewis A. Burke." The caption also offers the following: Hang Rock Point Lookout, Lookout Mountain Tennessee, Property of John Q. Tompkins, Photographed June 19, 1864. (loc)

enterprising professional photographers who followed the army to set up shop in Chattanooga. As a result, one of the most familiar themes in Civil War photography is that of a collection of uniformed men, posed on some outcropping atop Lookout Mountain.

Gen. D.C. McCallum and a "Capt. Hurlbut" seated on top of Lookout Mountain. (loc)

"Officers of the 16th U.S. Colored Troops Infantry Regiment"—The Library of Congress citation identifies the officers as Capt. Samuel Galloway, Lt. Jeremiah Chauncy, Lt. Charles W. Seidel, Lt. Lovett S. Rivenburg, Lt. William Jones, Lt. Joseph H. Barbour, and Lt. David H. Dickinson. (loc)

"Group of Officers on Lookout Mountain"—The Library of Congress citation identifies the men as 18th Ohio Infantry and15th Pennsylvania Cavalry. (loc)

Although the date of the photo and the identity of this group of boys remains unknown, the Library of Congress lists Royan M. Linn as the photographer, suggesting the photo was taken around the same time as Linn was photographing soldiers in this area. (loc)

Unidentified soldier in Union officer's uniform at Point Lookout, Tennessee, sitting with cavalry saber in hand and slouch hat resting beside him on a rock. Royan and James Birney Linn, photographers. (loc)

According to the Library of Congress: "Private Henry McCollum of Company B, 78th Pennsylvania Infantry Regiment and three unidentified soldiers in 78th Pennsylvania Infantry uniforms at Point Lookout, Tennessee." Royan M. Linn, photographer. (loc)

Three poses from Umbrella Rock capture different moods. Note in the third photo: one of the aluminum War Department signs. (loc)

CHATTANOOGA CAMPAIGN

NOVEMBER 12-25, 1863

units and commands on detached duty are not listed

OVERALL UNION FORCES
Maj. Gen. Ulysses S. Grant

ARMY OF THE CUMBERLAND
Maj. Gen. George H. Thomas

General Headquarters: *1st Ohio Sharpshooters • 10th Ohio Infantry*

FOURTH CORPS: Maj. Gen. Gordon Granger
FIRST DIVISION: Brig. Gen. Charles Cruft
Escort: *Co. E, 92nd Illinois Mounted Infantry*

Second Brigade: Brig. Gen. Walter C. Whitaker
96th Illinois • 35th Indiana • 8th Kentucky • 40th Ohio • 51st Ohio • 99th Ohio

Third Brigade: Col. William Grose
*59th Illinois • 75th Illinois • 84th Illinois • 9th Indiana • 36th Indiana
24th Ohio*

SECOND DIVISION: Maj. Gen. Philip Sheridan
First Brigade: Col. Francis T. Sherman
*36th Illinois • 44th Illinois • 73rd Illinois • 74th Illinois • 88th Illinois
22nd Indiana • 2nd Missouri • 15th Missouri • 24th Wisconsin*

Second Brigade: Brig. Gen. George D. Wagner
*100th Illinois • 15th Indiana • 40th Indiana • 51st Indiana • 57th Indiana
58th Indiana • 26th Ohio • 97th Ohio*

Third Brigade: Col. Charles G. Harker
*22nd Illinois • 27th Illinois • 42nd Illinois • 51st Illinois • 79th Illinois
3rd Kentucky • 64th Ohio • 65th Ohio • 125th Ohio*

Artillery: Capt. Warren P. Edgarton
*M, 1st Illinois Lt. • 10th Indiana Battery • G, 1st Missouri Lt. • I, 1st Ohio Lt.
G, 4th US • M, 4th US*

THIRD DIVISIOn: Brig. Gen. Thomas J. Wood
First Brigade: Brig. Gen. August Willich
*25th Illinois • 35th Illinois • 89th Illinois • 32nd Indiana • 68th Indiana
8th Kansas • 15th Ohio • 49th Ohio • 15th Wisconsin*

Second Brigade: Brig. Gen. William B. Hazen
*6th Indiana • 5th Kentucky • 6th Kentucky • 23rd Kentucky • 1st Ohio
6th Ohio • 41st Ohio • 93rd Ohio • 124th Ohio*

Third Brigade: Brig. Gen. Samuel Beatty
*79th Indiana • 86th Indiana • 9th Kentucky • 17th Kentucky • 13th Ohio
19th Ohio • 59th Ohio*

Artillery: Capt. Cullen Bradley
*Bridges's Battery, Illinois Lt. • 6th Ohio Battery • 20th Ohio Battery
B, Pennsylvania Lt.*

ELEVENTH CORPS: Maj. Gen. Oliver O. Howard
Independent Company: *8th New York Infantry*
SECOND DIVISION: Brig. Gen. Adolph von Steinwehr
First Brigade: Col. Adolphus Buschbeck
*33rd New Jersey • 134th New York • 154th New York • 27th Pennsylvania
73rd Pennsylvania*

Second Brigade: Col. Orland Smith
33rd Massachusetts • 136th New York • 55th Ohio • 73rd Ohio

THIRD DIVISION: Maj. Gen. Carl Schurz
First Brigade: Brig. Gen. Hector Tyndale
101st Illinois • 45th New York • 143rd New York • 61st Ohio • 82nd Ohio

Second Brigade: Col. Wladimir Krzyzanowski
58th New York • 119th New York • 141st New York • 26th Wisconsin

Third Brigade: Col. Frederick Hecker
80th Illinois • 82nd Illinois • 68th New York • 75th Pennsylvania

Artillery: Maj. Thomas W. Osborn
*I, 1st New York Lt. • 13th New York Lt. • I, 1st Ohio Lt. • K, 1st Ohio Lt.
G, 4th US*

TWELFTH CORPS: (only one division present)
SECOND DIVISION: Brig. Gen. John W. Geary
First Brigade: Col. Charles Candy
*5th Ohio • 7th Ohio • 29th Ohio • 66th Ohio • 28th Pennsylvania
147th Pennsylvania*

Second Brigade: Col. George A. Cobham, Jr.
29th Pennsylvania • 109th Pennsylvania • 111th Pennsylvania

Third Brigade: Col. David Ireland
*60th New York • 78th New York • 102nd New York • 137th New York
149th New York*

Artillery: Maj. John A. Reynolds
E, Pennsylvania Lt. • K, 5th US

FOURTEENTH CORPS: Maj. Gen. John M. Palmer
Co. L, 1st Ohio Cavalry
FIRST DIVISION: Brig. Gen. Richard W. Johnson
First Brigade: Brig. Gen. William P. Carlin
*104th Illinois • 38th Indiana • 42nd Indiana • 88th Indiana • 2nd Ohio
33rd Ohio • 94th Ohio • 10th Wisconsin*

Second Brigade: Col. Marshall F. Moore
19th Illinois • 11th Michigan • 69th Ohio • 1/15th US • 2/15th US
1/16th US • 1/18th US • 2/18th US • 1/19th US

Third Brigade: Brig. Gen. John C. Starkweather
24th Illinois • 37th Indiana • 21st Ohio • 74th Ohio • 78th Pennsylvania
79th Pennsylvania • 1st Wisconsin • 21st Wisconsin

Artillery: *C, 1st Illinois Lt • A, 1st Michigan Lt. • H, 5th US[1]*

SECOND DIVISION: Brig. Gen. Jefferson C. Davis
First Brigade: Brig. Gen. James D. Morgan
10th Illinois • 16th Illinois • 60th Illinois • 21st Kentucky • 10th Michigan

Second Brigade: Brig. Gen. John Beatty
34th Illinois • 78th Illinois • 98th Ohio • 108th Ohio • 113th Ohio
121st Ohio

Third Brigade: Col. Daniel McCook
85th Illinois • 86th Illinois • 110th Illinois • 125th Illinois • 52nd Ohio

Artillery: Capt. William A. Hotchkiss
I, 2nd Illinois Lt. • 2nd Minnesota Lt. • 5th Wisconsin Lt.

THIRD DIVISION: Brig. Gen. Absalom Baird
First Brigade: Brig. Gen. John B. Turchin
82nd Indiana • 11th Ohio • 17th Ohio • 31st Ohio • 36th Ohio
89th Ohio • 92nd Ohio

Second Brigade: Col. Ferdinand Van Derveer
75th Indiana • 87th Indiana • 101st Indiana • 2nd Minnesota • 9th Ohio
35th Ohio • 105th Ohio

Third Brigade: Col. Edward Phelps
10th Indiana • 74th Indiana • 4th Kentucky • 10th Kentucky
18th Kentucky • 14th Ohio • 38th Ohio

---

1 Temporarily attached to Sheridan's division of the Fourth Corps.

Artillery: Capt. George R. Swallow
7th Indiana Lt. • *19th Indiana Lt.* • *I, 4th US*

ENGINEER TROOPS: Brig. Gen. William F. Smith
1st Michigan Engineers (detachment) • *13th Michigan* • *21st Michigan*
22nd Michigan • *18th Ohio*

ARTILLERY RESERVE: Brig. Gen. John M. Brannan
FIRST DIVISION: Col. James Barnett
First Brigade: Maj. Charles S. Cotter
B, 1st Ohio Lt. • *C, 1st Ohio Lt.* • *E, 1st Ohio Lt.* • *F, 1st Ohio Lt.*

Second Brigade: (no commander listed)
G, 1st Ohio Lt. • *M, 1st Ohio Lt.* • *19th Ohio Battery* • *20th Ohio Battery*

SECOND DIVISION: (no commander listed)
First Brigade: Capt. Josiah W. Church
D, 1st Michigan Lt. • *A, 1st Tennessee Lt.* • *3rd Wisconsin Lt.*
8th Wisconsin Lt. • *10th Wisconsin Lt.*

Second Brigade: Capt. Arnold Sutermeister
4th Indiana Lt. • *8th Indiana Lt.* • *11th Indiana Lt.* • *21st Indiana Lt.*
C, 1st Wisconsin Heavy Artillery

CAVALRY CORPS: (mostly not present)
Second Brigade, Second Division: Col. Eli Long
98th Illinois Mounted Infantry • *17th Indiana Mounted Infantry*
2nd Kentucky Cavalry • *4th Michigan Cavalry* • *1st Ohio Cavalry*
3rd Ohio Cavalry • *Battalion* • *4th Ohio Cavalry* • *10th Ohio Cavalry*

POST OF CHATTANOOGA: Col. John G. Parkhurst
44th Indiana • *15th Kentucky* • *9th Michigan*

ARMY OF THE TENNESSEE
Maj. Gen. William T. Sherman

FIFTEENTH CORPS: Maj. Gen. Frank P. Blair
FIRST DIVISION: Brig. Gen. Peter J. Osterhaus
First Brigade: Brig. Gen. Charles R. Woods
*13th Illinois • 3rd Missouri • 12th Missouri • 17th Missouri • 27th Missouri
29th Missouri • 31st Missouri • 32nd Missouri • 76th Ohio*

Second Brigade: Col. James A. Williamson
4th Iowa • 9th Iowa • 25th Iowa • 26th Iowa • 30th Iowa • 31st Iowa

Artillery: Capt. Henry A. Griffiths
1st Iowa Lt. • F, 2nd Missouri Lt. • 4th Ohio Lt.

SECOND DIVISION: Brig. Gen. Morgan L. Smith
First Brigade: Brig. Gen. Giles A. Smith
*55th Illinois • 116th Illinois • 127th Illinois • 6th Missouri • 8th Missouri
57th Ohio • 1/13th US*

Second Brigade: Brig. Gen. Joseph A. Lightburn
*83rd Indiana • 30th Ohio • 37th Ohio • 47th Ohio • 54th Ohio
4th West Virginia*

Artillery: (no commander listed)
A, 1st Illinois Lt. • B, 1st Illinois Lt. • H, 1st Illinois Lt.

FOURTH DIVISION: Brig. Gen. Hugh Ewing
First Brigade: Col. John M. Loomis
26th Illinois • 90th Illinois • 12th Indiana • 100th Indiana

Second Brigade: Brig. Gen. John M. Corse
40th Illinois • 103rd Illinois • 6th Iowa • 46th Ohio

Third Brigade: Col. Joseph R. Cockerill
48th Illinois • 97th Indiana • 99th Indiana • 53rd Ohio • 70th Ohio

Artillery: Capt. Henry Richardson
F, 1st Illinois Lt. • I, 1st Illinois Lt. • D, 1st Missouri Lt.

SEVENTEENTH CORPS: (no commander listed)
SECOND DIVISION: Brig. Gen. John E. Smith
First Brigade: Col. Jesse I. Alexander
63rd Illinois • 48th Indiana • 59th Indiana • 4th Minnesota
18th Wisconsin

Second Brigade: Col. Green B. Raum
56th Illinois • 17th Iowa • 10th Missouri • 24th Missouri • 80th Ohio

Third Brigade: Brig. Gen. Charles L. Matthies
93rd Illinois • 5th Iowa • 10th Iowa • 26th Missouri

Artillery: Capt. Henry Dillon
Cogswell's Illinois Battery • 6th Wisconsin Lt. • 12th Wisconsin Lt.

*   *   *

CONFEDERATE ARMY OF TENNESSEE
(Organization shown from November 12, 1863)
Gen. Braxton Bragg

General Headquarters: *1st Louisiana Infantry (regulars) • 1st Louisiana Cavalry*

LONGSTREET'S CORPS: Lt. Gen. James Longstreet[2]
McLAWS'S DIVISION: Maj. Gen. Lafayette McLaws
Kershaw's Brigade: Brig. Gen. Joseph B. Kershaw
2nd South Carolina • 3rd South Carolina • 7th South Carolina
8th South Carolina • 15th South Carolina • 3rd South Carolina Battalion

Humphreys's Brigade: Brig. Gen. Benjamin C. Humphreys
13th Mississippi • 17th Mississippi • 18th Mississippi • 21st Mississippi

---

2 From Virginia, detached to East Tennessee in early November

Wofford's Brigade: Col. S. Z. Ruff
16th Georgia • 18th Georgia • 24th Georgia • Cobb's Legion
3rd Georgia Battalion Sharpshooters

Bryan's Brigade: Brig. Gen. Goode Bryan
10th Georgia • 50th Georgia • 51st Georgia • 53rd Georgia

Artillery: Maj. Austin Leyton
Peeples's Georgia Battery • Wolihin's Georgia Battery • York's Georgia Battery

HOOD'S DIVISION: Brig. Gen. Micah Jenkins
Jenkins's Brigade: Col. John Bratton
1st South Carolina • 2nd South Carolina Rifles • 5th South Carolina
6th South Carolina • Hampton Legion • Palmetto Sharpshooters

Law's Brigade: Brig. Gen. Evander M. Law
4th Alabama • 15th Alabama • 44th Alabama • 47th Alabama
48th Alabama

Robertson's Brigade: Brig. Gen. Jerome B. Robertson
3rd Arkansas • 1st Texas • 4th Texas • 5th Texas

Anderson's Brigade: Brig. Gen. George T. Anderson
7th Georgia • 8th Georgia • 9th Georgia • 11th Georgia • 59th Georgia

Benning's Brigade: Brig. Gen. Henry L. Benning
2nd Georgia • 15th Georgia • 17th Georgia • 20th Georgia

Artillery: Col. E. Porter Alexander
*Fickling's South Carolina Battery • Jordan's Virginia Battery • Moody's
Louisiana Battery • Parker's Virginia Battery • Taylor's Virginia Battery
Woolfolk's Virginia Battery*

HARDEE'S CORPS: Lt. Gen. William J. Hardee
CHEATHAM'S DIVISION: Maj. Gen. William H. T. Walker
Jackson's Brigade: Brig. Gen. John K. Jackson
1st Georgia • 5th Georgia • 47th Georgia • 65th Georgia
2nd Battalion Georgia Sharpshooters • 5th Mississippi • 8th Mississippi

Moore's Brigade: Brig. Gen. John C. Moore
37th Alabama • 40th Alabama • 42nd Alabama

Walthall's Brigade: Brig. Gen. Edward C. Walthall
24th Mississippi • 27th Mississippi • 29th Mississippi • 30th Mississippi
34th Mississippi

Wright's Brigade: Brig. Gen. Marcus J. Wright
8th Tennessee • 16th Tennessee • 28th Tennessee • 38th Tennessee
51st/52nd Tennessee • Murray's Tennessee Battalion

Artillery: Maj. Melancton Smith
Fowler's Alabama Battery • McCants's Florida Battery • Scogin's Georgia Battery
Turner's (Smith's) Mississippi Battery

HINDMAN'S DIVISION: Brig. Gen. J. Patton Anderson
Anderson's Brigade: Col. William F. Tucker
7th Mississippi • 9th Mississippi • 10th Mississippi • 41st Mississippi
44th Mississippi • 9th Mississippi Battalion Sharpshooters

Manigault's Brigade: Brig. Gen. Arthur M. Manigault
24th Alabama • 28th Alabama • 34th Alabama • 10th/19th South Carolina

Deas's Brigade: Brig. Gen. Zachariah C. Deas
19th Alabama • 22nd Alabama • 25th Alabama • 33rd Alabama
50th Alabama • 17th Alabama Battalion Sharpshooters

Vaughan's Brigade: Brig. Gen. Alfred J. Vaughan, Jr.
11th Tennessee • 12th/47th Tennessee • 13th/154th Tennessee • 29th Tennessee

Artillery: Maj. Alfred R. Courtney
Dent's Alabama Battery • Garrity's Alabama Battery • Doscher's (Scott's)
Tennessee Battery • Hamilton's (Water's) Alabama Battery

BUCKNER'S DIVISION: Brig. Gen. Bushrod R. Johnston[3]
Johnson's Brigade: Col. John S. Fulton
17th/23rd Tennessee • 25th/44th Tennessee • 63rd Tennessee

---

3 This division, except for Reynolds's brigade and the artillery, was sent to East Tennessee on November 22.

Gracie's Brigade: Brig. Gen. Archibald Gracie, Jr.
41st Alabama • 43rd Alabama, 1st, 2nd, 3rd, & 4th Battalions
Hilliard's (Alabama) Legion

Reynolds's Brigade: Brig. Gen. A. W. Reynolds (attached to Stevenson's division after November 22)
58th North Carolina • 60th North Carolina • 54th Virginia • 63rd Virginia

Artillery: Maj. Samuel C. Williams
Bullen's (Darden's) Mississippi Battery • Jeffries's Virginia Battery
Kolb's Alabama Battery

WALKER'S DIVISION: Brig. Gen. States Rights Gist
Maney's Brigade: Brig. Gen. George Maney
1st/27th Tennessee • 4th Tennessee • 6th/9th Tennessee • 41st Tennessee
56th Tennessee • 24th Tennessee Battalion Sharpshooters

Gist's Brigade: Col. James McCullough
46th Georgia • 8th Georgia Battalion • 16th South Carolina • 24th South Carolina

Wilson's Brigade: Col. Claudius C. Wilson
25th Georgia • 29th Georgia • 30th Georgia • 26th Georgia Battalion
1st Georgia Battalion Sharpshooters

Artillery: Maj. Robert Martin
Bledsoe's Missouri Battery • Ferguson's South Carolina Battery
Howell's Georgia Battery

BRECKINRIDGE'S CORPS: Maj. Gen. John C. Breckinridge
CLEBURNE'S DIVISION: Maj. Gen. Patrick R. Cleburne
Liddell's Brigade: Col. Daniel C. Govan
2nd/15th Arkansas • 5th/13th Arkansas • 6th/7th Arkansas
19th/24th Arkansas

Smith's Brigade: Col. Hiram B. Granbury
6th/10th Texas Infantry/15th Texas Dismounted Cavalry • 7th Texas Infantry
17th/18th/24th/25th Texas Dismounted Cavalry

Polk's Brigade: Brig. Gen. Lucius Polk
1st Arkansas • *3rd/5th Confederate* • *2nd Tennessee* • *35th/48th Tennessee*

Lowrey's Brigade: Brig. Gen. Mark P. Lowrey
16th Alabama • *33rd Alabama* • *45th Alabama* • *32nd/45th Mississippi*
15th Mississippi Battalion Sharpshooters

Artillery: *Key's Arkansas Battery* • *Douglas's Texas Battery*
Goldthwaite's (Semple's) Alabama Battery • *Shannon's (Swett's) Mississippi Battery*

STEWART'S DIVISION: Maj. Gen. Alexander P. Stewart
Adam's Brigade: Col. Randall L. Gibson
13th/20th Louisiana • *16th/25th Louisiana* • *19th Louisiana*
4th Louisiana Battalion • *14th Louisiana Battalion Sharpshooters*

Strahl's Brigade: Brig. Gen. Otho F. Strahl
4th/5th Tennessee • *18th Tennessee* • *24th Tennessee* • *31st Tennessee*
33rd Tennessee

Clayton's Brigade: Col. J. T. Holtzclaw
18th Alabama • *32nd Alabama* • *36th Alabama* • *38th Alabama*
58th Alabama

Stovall's Brigade: Brig. Gen. Marcellus A. Stovall
40th Georgia • *41st Georgia* • *42nd Georgia* • *43rd Georgia* • *52nd Georgia*

Artillery: Capt. Henry C. Semple
Anderson's (Dawson's) Georgia Battery • *Rivers's (Humphreys's) Arkansas*
Battery • *Oliver's Alabama Battery* • *Stanford's Mississippi Battery*

BRECKINRIDGE'S DIVISION: Maj. Gen. William B. Bate
Lewis's Brigade: Brig. Gen. Joseph H. Lewis
2nd Kentucky • *4th Kentucky* • *5th Kentucky* • *6th Kentucky*
8th Kentucky • *Morgan's detachment dismounted Cavalry*

Bate's Brigade: Col. R. C. Tyler
37th Georgia • *4th Georgia Battalion Sharpshooters* • *10th Tennessee*
15th/37th Tennessee • *20th Tennessee* • *30th Tennessee* • *1st Tennessee Battalion*

Florida Brigade: Col. Jesse J. Finley
1st/3rd Florida • 4th Florida • 6th Florida • 7th Florida
1st Florida Dismounted Cavalry

Artillery: Capt. C. H. Slocomb
Gracey's (Cobb's) Kentucky Battery • Mebane's Tennessee Battery • Vaught's
(Slocomb's) Louisiana Battery

STEVENSON'S DIVISION: Maj. Gen. Carter L. Stevenson
Brown's Brigade: Brig. Gen. John C. Brown
3rd Tennessee • 18th/20th Tennessee • 32nd Tennessee • 45th Tennessee
23rd Tennessee Battalion

Cumming's Brigade: Brig. Gen. Alfred Cumming
34th Georgia • 36th Georgia • 39th Georgia • 56th Georgia

Pettus's Brigade: Brig. Gen. Edmund W. Pettus
20th Alabama • 23rd Alabama • 30th Alabama • 31st Alabama • 46th
Alabama

Artillery: Capt. Robert Cobb
Baxter's Tennessee Battery • Carnes's Tennessee Battery • Van Den Corput's
Georgia Battery • Rowan's Georgia Battery

CAVALRY[4]
KELLY'S DIVISION: Brig. Gen. John H. Kelly
First Brigade: Col. William B. Wade
1st Confederate • 3rd Confederate • 8th Confederate • 10th Confederate

Second Brigade: Col. J. Warren Grigsby
2nd Kentucky • 3rd Kentucky • 9th Kentucky • Allison's Tennessee Squadron
Hamilton's Tennessee Battalion • Rucker's Legion

Artillery: (no commander listed)
Huggins's Tennessee Battery • Huwald's Tennessee Battery • White's Tennessee
Battery • Wiggins's Arkansas Battery

---

4 The bulk of Maj. Gen. Joseph Wheeler's Cavalry Corps was operating in East Tennessee, first with Stevenson, then with Longstreet. Only Kelly's division remained with Bragg, and of that force, Kelly and Wade's brigade was operating around Cleveland Tennessee.

$\mathcal{S}$uggested $\mathcal{R}$eading

The Shipwreck of Their Hopes: The Battles for Chattanooga
Peter Cozzens
University of Illinois, 1994
ISBN: 0-252-01922-9

Peter Cozzens's study of the campaign is very tactical, with a tight focus on regimental movements and actions. It is the third book of three focusing on the campaigns of the Army of the Cumberland. His focus here remains primarily on that army, though he does not skimp in detailing the actions of either the Confederates or of those Federals brought in to reinforce the Army of the Cumberland.

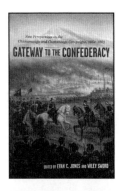

Gateway to the Confederacy: New Perspectives on the Chickamauga and Chattanooga Campaigns, 1862-1863
Evan C. Jones and Wiley Sword, eds.
Louisiana State University, 2014
ISBN: 978-0-8071-5509-7

The Chattanooga Campaign
Steven E. Woodworth and Charles D. Grear, eds.
Southern Illinois University Press, 2012
ISBN: 978-0-8093-3119-5

Each of these last two books are essay collections, not narrative histories of the campaigns in question. Each volume includes ten chapters penned by different experts. The insights offered range from the pondering of campaign considerations to explorations of Civil War memory and preservation; taken together they richly reward the reader with some of the best short historical writing on the subject of Chattanooga.

Mountains Touched with Fire:
Chattanooga Besieged, 1863
Wiley Sword
St. Martin's Press, 1995
ISBN: 0-312-11859-7

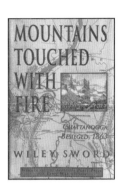

Wiley Sword's study of the same conflict, appearing the year after Cozzens's work, is focused a bit more on the upper echelons of command for both sides; it is more of an operational study than a tactical one. Both volumes offer valuable insights into the events known collectively as the Chattanooga campaign, but perhaps Sword's language is slightly more lyrical and evocative.

Six Armies in Tennessee: The Chickamauga and
Chattanooga Campaigns
Steven E. Woodworth
University of Nebraska, 1998
ISBN: 0-8032-4778-8

Steven Woodworth's narrative is a high-level strategic and operational view of the entire struggle, beginning with the Tullahoma campaign in June 1863 and concluding with the Confederate defeat at Chattanooga at the end of November. In covering such a broad sweep in less than 250 pages, Woodworth's narrative remains focused on decision-making within the upper echelons of command, but his insight into those decisions make this book essential for comprehending the strategic narrative.

Bushwhacking on a Grand Scale: The Battle of
Chickamauga, September 18-20, 1863
William Lee White
Savas Beatie, 2013 (Emerging Civil War Series)
ISBN: 978-1-61121-158-0

The battle for Lookout Mountain was but one part of a larger story: the months-long struggle for control of Chattanooga. The Chickamauga campaign was the first part of that story. *Bushwhacking on a Grand Scale* serves as a worthy introduction to that campaign, which culminated in the second-largest battle of the Civil War and helps to explain some of the earlier strategic decisions surrounding the fighting for Chattanooga.

About the Author

David Powell is the author of five books on the Chickamauga Campaign: *The Maps of Chickamauga, Failure in the Saddle,* and a three-volume narrative—*A Mad, Irregular Battle; Flory or the Grave;* and *Barren Victory,* all published by Savas Beatie. He is a two-time winner of the Atlanta Civil War Round Table's prestigious Harwell Award, and is nationally recognized for his tours of the battles around Chattanooga. A 1983 graduate of the Virgina Military Institute, by day he runs a courier company in the greater Chicago metro area.

Dave is working on a companion volume to this work, *Missionary Ridge,* which will conclude the battles for Chattanooga for the Emerging Civil War Series.